I Do My Best Work Behind the Scenes

A Guide to Powerful Demonstrations

By

Cath DePalma

I Do My Best Work Behind the Scenes: A Guide to Powerful Demonstrations

© 2024 By Cath DePalma

Published by Portal Center Press
Waldport, Oregon
www.portalcenterpress.com

ISBN: 978-1-936902-56-9

About the Cover

A Guide to Powerful Demonstrations

    A Japanese Maple was chosen for the cover in honor of my Cousin Walter who started me on this path. He adored them and planted them wherever he could. They symbolize calm, rest and peace. Trees have healing powers, and they are powerful symbols of growth, strength, resurrection, fresh starts in life, positive energy, good health and bright futures. Whenever I see them, I am reminded of him.

Dedication

I dedicate this book to my cousin, Dr. Walter Peach, who threw me a life-line when I needed it most. From his help and example, a stronger, healthier me emerged and a whole new life was born. Walter, I am forever grateful to you for being there for me and I know you continue to contribute to my life from the other side.

Contents

About the Cover	overleaf
Dedication	i
Introduction	vii
Special Notes to My Readers	x
Section I	1
Chapter One: What's It All About?	3
Chapter Two: The Great Awakening—Where It All Began!	6
Chapter Three: Inside Out World	10
1. Prioritize (above all else) Soundness of the Self	11
2. Follow Your Heart, Not Your Head	12
Chapter Four: Home Is Where It All Comes Together	13
BASECAMP PREPARATIONS FOR ORDER AND ORGANIZATION	15
Chapter Five: The Divine Setup	17
A Moment of Gratitude For My Mom...	17
A Moment of Gratitude For My Dad...	19
A Moment of Gratitude For My Siblings...	22
A Moment of Gratitude For Colette...	22
A Moment of Gratitude For Cynder...	23
A Moment of Gratitude For Nic & Liz...	23
A Moment of Gratitude For Cousin Walter...	25
A Moment of Gratitude For Ken...	25
A Moment of Gratitude For Carol...	27
A Moment of Gratitude For Ray...	28

A Moment of Gratitude For Sam... 29

A Moment of Gratitude For Fred... 30

Chapter Six: Spiritual Tools 32

Spiritual Tool: Affirmation 32

Spiritual Tool: Intention 33

Spiritual Tool: Meditation 34

Spiritual Tool: Visualization 35

Spiritual Tool: Visioning 35

Spiritual Tool: OMG!s 36

Spiritual Tool: Mind Treatment 37

Section II 41

Chapter Seven: John 43

Chapter Eight: A Calling 46

Chapter Nine: Joseph 49

Chapter Ten: A Retreat to the Canadian Rockies 54

Chapter Eleven: Africa Calls 58

Chapter Twelve: Community Outreach 67

Chapter Thirteen: The Great Blue Heron 73

The Cover of I Can Do This Thing Called Life: And So Can You! 74

The Cover of Energize Your Creative Super Powers, 7 Ways to Spiritual Fitness

75

Chapter Fourteen: A Spiritual Bookstore 78

Chapter Fifteen: 20th Anniversary 82

Section III 87

Chapter Sixteen: Leaving the Nest 89

Chapter Seventeen: An Alaskan Cruise 98

Technique: Small Shifts	100
Technique: Mutuality	101
Chapter Eighteen: Stepping Down	105
Chapter Nineteen: Back to Atlanta	111
Chapter Twenty: A Special Place to Be	117
Chapter Twenty-One: Full Circle	121
Sacred Space	121
Everything Serves	123
Shoot the Moon	124
The Hand of God	126
Closing Letter	129
Acknowledgements	133
About the Author	134
People, Movies and Books to Enlighten and Inspire	135
Addendum	**141**
My Ideal Day	142
Mind Treatment	144
Other Books by Cath DePalma	146

Introduction

"For the first time in human history we are required, as a species, to extend ourselves into radically new ways of being. The tasks that are now ours, the tasks of virtual creation, compel the revolution in consciousness that tells us that we are part of the great unfolding of Spirit in flesh. ...These are the times. We are the people..."

— Jean Houston's Foreword for *The Science of Mind*

One of the most difficult things we came here to do is have an up close and personal relationship with our inner being, the Source within us. This Source is such a natural part of our being we don't even know it exists. In our western culture it is easier to think we are our minds, our bodies, our personalities and our life experiences. What else is there? Our outward focus on our physicality and the world around us keeps us distracted from our true selves, and we lose sight of what is real. It often feels awkward, almost as if we are going against the grain, to recognize that there could possibly be more to us than meets the eye.

What does it even mean to have an inner being?

Where do we go with that?

My own spiritual journey began abruptly, following a heated discussion with my first husband. What started out like a normal day turned into a day from hell. The Midwest doesn't have volcanoes, but I felt like one that day as my core let loose.

To be fair, I hadn't been a picnic to live with either. For over a year, I had been coming to terms with the fact that my father, who had been a firefighter for the city of Milwaukee, was in a coma caused by a tragic accident on the job. I thought we would have him in our lives for a very long time, but this tragedy had turned our lives completely upside down. I cried every day for months knowing he would never be the same. Shortly after, my husband, a federal agent, was able to transfer to the Chicago office so we could be closer to my family. Leaving our life in Springfield and starting over in a large city wasn't easy. The drastic changes we underwent barely gave us a chance to catch our breath. On top of that, it was an election year and my husband was on the road every three weeks for three weeks. I was at home, in a new city with two small children, grieving, and trying to carry on. I realize now my explosion was a culmination of emotions that I'd been carrying, plus the information he shared about his own methods of coping with the stress of living a high-powered life on the road. Clearly our relationship was too far gone; the life we had together was over. Whatever bubble we were living in popped that day. Not long afterwards, a social worker reached out and shared that many of the agents' families were having trouble. I learned that whatever problems were already present in relationships escalate rapidly under the additional pressures and time away from home that were unavoidable in an election year. While it was comforting to know we were not alone in these difficulties, there was no going back for us.

I walked away from our conversation that day feeling like I had fallen into an abyss, with no possible way out. I had no idea that I was about to embark on a journey that would lead me into a whole new way of thinking and living. I thought a crash and burn meant there was no coming back. I was wrong. I would come back stronger than ever. I was awake.

Maybe you were, or currently are, in a situation where things aren't what you thought they were. Maybe you feel abandoned, rejected, misunderstood, or any of the other difficult extremes of emotion we feel as humans. Maybe you are in a scary place with yourself, feeling alone and not knowing which way to go. Maybe you don't even know you have options. Maybe you know you have options but are afraid of making another wrong turn. Maybe you think the average existence is as good as it gets. Or maybe life is going well, but you want to level up your experiences and open yourself up to the greater yet to be. Some people just know they want more out of their life and are interested in improving themselves without a disaster intervening and bringing them to their senses. Whatever it is that prevents you from seeing a way out of your discomfort or unrest, know that there is more life for you waiting to be enjoyed. I never thought I could ever be happy again, but I learned how to put my pain behind me by transforming it. I had no idea that a whole new world lay at my feet, waiting for me.

The first step for me was to admit that I was responsible for my experience. I was not a victim. Something greater was happening in me. When I got as real as I could with myself, I saw that in reality, it was I who had yearned for more and called it in. Part of my healing was forgiving us both. After all, we were only in our 20's.

Almost 10 years later, after much study and work on myself, I became a minister so that I could help others live from a place of greater spiritual strength. As a co-director of the Central Florida Center for Spiritual Living, with my new husband, John, I had plenty of opportunities to teach and deepen my own understanding of the Universal Principles through personal practice. Over the course of my 25 years at the center, we mentored hundreds of individuals from many different backgrounds while co-parenting our children and having a baby together. Demonstrating, time and time again, encouraged me to share what I've observed and learned with others in my books *I Can Do This Thing Called Life and So Can You, Energize Your Creative Super Powers, 7 Ways to Spiritual Fitness*, (a workbook to the first book), and now in this one.

Today I live an exceptional life, where I collaborate with the Infinite on the kind of life I want to live. Mysterious things happen—things I would never have noticed before happen all the time. Not because I am special, but rather because I now see the world from a different vantage point. I am on the lookout for the unusual, the seemingly magical, and the extraordinary. Experience has led me to a greater awareness and a clearer understanding, which give me a different perspective. Coming from a healthier love opens me up and gives me a larger capacity to receive what I couldn't before. My spiritual practice and philosophy of life help me keep the door open to Spirit and ITs incredibly amazing works all around me, from a momma bear and cub crossing my path while we lived in Orlando, Florida, to having a peacock, of all things, show up at my front door. From feeling better about myself all the time, to discovering my own self-worth. I love having an up close and personal relationship with Source. Life presents me with things that make me happy. I feel extremely supported, and I finally feel like I belong here.

In *I Do My Best Work Behind the Scenes*, you will learn that everything begins with you—that it is an inside-out world and not an outside-in one. Getting in touch with your spiritual nature and how life really works makes a world of difference. You will get the Behind-the-Scenes scoop on the creation of some of my best demonstrations, accomplished with nothing but a clear intention and powerful mind treatments.

What about you? Are you ready to receive your own version of what makes you happy? Are you calling for change and expansion in your life? Are you ready to see things you couldn't see before? Let's take a closer look Behind the Scenes, and see this whole other universe that awaits us all. Are you ready? With a little bit of help, you, too, will be on your way to a new kind of life.

Special Notes to My Readers

Whether we call it Buddha, Allah, Spirit, Life, God, Energy, Infinite Mind, Intelligence, Source, Love, Good, or anything I have not included, we are really talking about the same Entity. IT is the same Power and Presence that works with us all. There is only One, and we are all really living the One Life of Spirit together. How can anyone's idea of God be better than another's when we are describing the same God? Is it possible for any of us to understand an infinite God? Hardly, and yet, there is no reason why we shouldn't try. There is much we can learn in the attempt.

Throughout the book, I use different names for God. One name hardly describes the Ultimate Thing Itself. While most people recognize the word God, there are probably as many different interpretations of what God is as there are people. God is beyond names, really. Sometimes I refer to our Source as IT, not out of disrespect in any way, but to get us to expand our idea of God as a personality. Personality implies that God, like us, has an ego, limitations, moods and judgment calls. This explains why we feel that God works for us sometimes but not others.

In this book, we will honor IT, The Thing ITself—a phrase coined by Ernest Holmes—by varying ITs name in an attempt to eliminate the inherent gender aspect given to the traditional western God, the Ultimate Stuff out of which all Life is made, the One, God, or Source of us all by varying the name.

We can still have a personal relationship with the God of our understanding by whatever name we use and feel a connection with. The God we are talking about goes beyond anything we can imagine, yet it is up to us to stretch our minds to a larger concept of what IT is so we can become more god-like and work alongside this Creative Intelligence, as a partner. This Intelligence, this Divine and Perfect Love, will respond to us in a way that allows us to feel a connection with IT. We can each have an up-close and personal relationship with our Source, which is always available to us because IT is closer than our very breath.

Love and Law are the two aspects of God, Spirit, Life. For a fuller and more comprehensive understanding of what our Source is, it is important to avoid limiting ourselves to either one: a God of Love or a God of Law. Both sides need to be taken into consideration. This way we know we are all loved and are all treated fairly and supported, even if we don't quite understand all the laws of the Universe yet.

Some of my favorite references to God are sprinkled throughout the book. My purpose is to familiarize the reader with looking at God in more than one way. Here is my list:

Source, Spirit, Universe, Infinite Intelligence, The Tao, Cosmic Intelligence, Life, Good, Truth, Love and Law, Energy, Universal Mind, Presence, Higher Power, IT, The Thing Itself. Principle, The Infinite, Universal Principles, God

Whatever name puts you in touch with the divine is most meaningful for you to use. It is all the same thing and so there is no right or wrong name. We honor and respect whatever name you choose.

In Chapter 6 on Spiritual Tools, we will discuss different spiritual practices and ideas that you can use regularly to engage in a deeper, more satisfying relationship with yourself and Life. Before we get there, you will notice that I use the word *treatment* or the phrases *mind treatment* or *prayer treatment* interchangeably. They are synonymous terms referring to a form of affirmative prayer. Affirmative prayer claims that we already have our desire before we actually see it. We pray differently from how many of us have been taught, as Jesus instructed when he said, "Pray believing." Treatment is not begging, beseeching or even bargaining with God. It aligns us with our Source making it possible to see what is already here for us. By focusing this way, we call our desire into existence. Mind treatment is a step-by-step tool for shifting consciousness and moving our minds in a more favorable direction. Mind treatment takes us beyond commonplace thinking and puts us in touch with a much larger, more inclusive perspective. For now, whenever I use words relating to treatment, this is the process I am referring to.

Next, this workbook is for YOU!

I know some readers will be ready to dive into the exercises right away, but I highly recommend reading through the entire book first to become familiar with the different ways to incorporate more spirituality into your life. Some already have a spiritual practice and are looking for ways to go deeper. Others are brand new to this idea and just getting started. Either way, this book is for everyone! From our new place, we can begin to take steps and make choices from the selections here that are perfect for our individual situations. And if you can't help yourself and feel called to dive right in, that is okay, too! Listen to your inner guide, as it knows you best and always knows what is right for you.

Remember, this is a lifelong journey. Introducing new ideas and outlooks requires big adjustments in us. There is no reason to hurry. Part of the path is being kinder and more loving to ourselves, even if it is difficult at first. Be as lighthearted as you can be and enjoy the unfoldment of something wonderful!

Section I

The Rehearsal

Chapter One: What's It All About?

"We are in a freefall into the future. We don't know where we're going. Things are changing so fast, and always when you're going through a long tunnel, anxiety comes along. And all you have to do to transform your hell into a paradise is to turn your fall into a voluntary act. It's a very interesting shift of perspective and that's all it is...joyful participation in the sorrows and everything changes."

— Joseph Campbell

What an exhilarating time to be alive! Times like this are not for the faint of heart, are they? They require strength of character, flexibility, and adaptability. More essential than ever is having a strong connection to that which is greater than ourselves—a higher power by whatever name you call it—in order for us to not only survive but to thrive. Living today requires an understanding and a belief that, while things on the outside appear to be falling apart, something greater is being revealed from within.

For years now, my husband has said: "Okay, we are awake already. What's next?"

It's a great question. What is next? Having survived a global pandemic, we are now more awake as a species than ever before. A huge shift has taken place in our global consciousness, bringing our most daunting fears and emotions to the surface, and forcing us to address things that we had long since buried, denied, or just plain didn't know what to do with. Now, every move we make reminds us that we are in this together and that we have to act with love and compassion for ourselves and each other in order to succeed as a species. What we are experiencing now is just the beginning of a forever, life-changing journey to where we need to go.

While awakenings certainly build our character, deepen us, and allow us to grow into more, they can also be difficult, painful and sometimes gut-wrenching. There's a lot of work involved with growing into, and eventually becoming, a divine human. Yes, there are many steps to this unfoldment! Yes, they include trials and tribulations! But there are never hardships demanded of us out of spite, or at random. Life doesn't work that way. There are consequences to our actions, but never punishments. We attract what we are and what we believe in. It really is all about mastering our own minds.

Will our problems be gone forever if we take the steps we need to take? Not necessarily. Problems in and of themselves are not the real issue. What looks like a problem to the untrained eye is merely an opportunity for improvement. Obstacles are necessary for evolution to occur. Once we take the stigma off of them and see them as something greater trying to happen, we can move forward through the new doors that will open. There will always be more creative solutions to find and memorable experiences to be had. Problems are our friends, not our roadblocks—opportunities to create again from a stronger vantage point.

Facing our challenges puts us in a better position to work through our old worn-out ways of doing things and unpack any unnecessary baggage we have accumulated along the way. After that, we can spend more of our precious time knowing we are the ones we have been waiting for. Hidden within us is the very power we seek. All around us, the Intelligence of the Universe exists—we sit basking in this immense power and presence.

Admittedly, change is not always easy. It takes getting used to, especially at the rapid rate at which we now experience it. There are specific skills and consciousness-raising tactics that we have to develop in order to move forward into the next iteration of ourselves and our lives. Each one of us is on our own path, specially designed for our benefit. Each of us is on a course, exquisitely laid out and orchestrated by an Infinite Intelligence, that knows us intimately and presents us with everything we need to live a full, rich life. Our Source, our innermost being, has the means to love and care for us in a way that is unique to each of us. Similar to the observations of Gary Chapman in his book *The Five Love Languages*, about the existence of more than one 'language of love', the Universe knows the language that speaks to *our* hearts in particular. If we can get ourselves straight with what is really going on, nurture ourselves, and trust that everything happening is for good, we can begin to see that a transformation is underway. As we realize this, we can learn to move with it. We can stand in awe and wonder, right smack-dab in the middle of changes, and know we are moving in the direction we need to go.

The truth is that you are stronger, more resilient, and more capable than you may realize. You are a unique expression of Life. There is no one exactly like you in all the Universe. Each one of us is divinely designed by the Creator of us all. We were first an idea in the Divine Mind and now we have been born into the physical world to have a human experience.

It helps to know that the larger part of us is still non-physical. Some might call it intuition, others our guardian angel and still others, the still small voice within us that speaks. That presence is always there even though we might not hear it. It is our source, our strength, our power—that part of us that is not affected by anything we experience here in the physical realm. Where does that leave me—the only self I know?

Imagine with me a delicious pie, representing everything you have going for you. Our physical self, the self you know, is like a small slice of that pie. The great unseen within you is the rest of the pie—your navigational system, your inner guide, your inner knowing, the vastness of power and potential within you that awaits your recognition of it.

There is that within us all that awaits our recognition and awareness. It waits until we are ready, until we invite it to be a part of our lives. That happening is a significant turning point in our lives because now we are working with that part of us which is infinite, that knows no bounds. Jesus said it this way: "The Father within me does the works." What he was saying is that the larger part of him that is not seen does the parts that he, in and of himself, cannot do. We come into this life with that very same strength and power within us that goes beyond what we know. Once we recognize that presence and power within us and let it in, we have access to what it can do beyond what we can do as only one small piece of the pie. That's when we have the whole thing working on our behalf. Believe me, that is a game changer! Focusing on just what we outwardly see ourselves to be makes us think we are in this world alone. From that point of view, we have to do everything by ourselves. When we learn that we could never be alone or cut off from our Source, that all of life is conspiring on our behalf, then we have more going for us than we know. Through spiritual practices, we can get to know and learn to work with the total package that is us. From there, we can create together so that we may live the exceptional lives we were created to live and enjoy all life has to offer.

Today, there are more ideas for us to play with than ever before in the history of the human race. Synchronicities abound. There are more choices, varieties, options, and contrasts to sort through, leading us to greater clarity through our focus. Clarity puts us in direct alignment with the kind of results that entice us to play our part in the Creative Process. Solutions we never even thought possible are beginning to surface, revealing the perfection of the Infinite Intelligence that permeates all. The question we have to ask ourselves is this: am I ready to leave the old world with its outdated, limiting ideas behind? There is so much potential for greater satisfaction, fulfillment, and happiness when we do.

No matter what is going on with you, no matter what you are going through, it is time to celebrate who you are and see the situation you are facing for the gift it is. I am not saying you will not have to work through your feelings. We should, with proper help, face our shadows. There is an intelligent reordering of things for the sole purpose of making our lives freer and easier. Everything serves. Everything has a purpose. Growth and expansion are the way forward. Whether we know it or not, we have been asking for more, and more is here, ready to come into our lives, just waiting for us to be ready. It is comforting to know the presence of the Quantum Field (God, Spirit, Intelligence, Life, Field of Potentiality, whatever you call it), the way IT works, what IT does, and that IT is always here for us. This force will gladly take us to new heights if we just let IT. There is no end to what IT can and will do for us.

Chapter Two: The Great Awakening—Where It All Began!

"There is a river flowing now very fast. It is so great and swift, that there are those who will be afraid. They will try to hold on to the shore, they will feel they are being torn apart and will suffer greatly. Know that the river has its destination. The elders say I must let go of the shore, push off into the middle of the river, keep my eyes open and my head above the water. And I say see who is there with me and celebrate. At this time in history, I AM to take nothing personally, least of all myself, for the moment that I do, my spiritual growth and journey come to a halt. The time of the lone wolf is over. Gather myself. Banish the word struggle from my attitude and vocabulary. All that I do now must be done in a sacred manner and in celebration...I AM the one I have been waiting for."

— Words of a Hopi Elder

My own awakening took place almost 40 years ago. My life had completely fallen apart. I was stuck in the muck and mire. How did this happen? I had always dreamt of so much more. This couldn't possibly be my fate—could it? Do I deserve this? Am I a bad person?

Therapy helped me air out these feelings, and I was ready to move on for good, but I had no idea how to go about facilitating such a powerful change. *What is my best next step?* A voice within urged me to call my cousin Walter. He happened to live in Atlanta, the city I'd just moved to, and it had been years since we last talked. Despite their infrequency, our talks were a safe space for us both to open up. At the time, the vast majority of our communication had taken place at family gatherings, but the conversations were unlike any you might associate with such an event. Even if we started with small talk, we would instinctively find our way into intellectually stimulating discussions about religion and philosophical theory nearly every time. Now, I needed a lifeline. Something told me that he was it.

I wasn't sure what he could do to help, I just knew I had to call him. At first, I questioned his recommendation of a church (that would soon become a Center for Spiritual Living), but I was in no position to turn down an idea. It was a conclusion that I probably would have never come to on my own, but I had to stay open. After all, this is exactly what I'd asked for. I decided to give it a try.

Not just any church would do, though. Prior to this, I had no real hope of ever 'being saved' by a Divine Power. By that, I don't mean I was worried about my relationship with God. I was never worried about God. I saw God differently than most. By 'saved', I mean miraculously freed from the reality I felt trapped in. At the time, I could've easily spent the rest of my life *trying* to make peace with the past, *trying* to have some kind of relationship with my children, *trying* to trust myself again. And that absolutely terrified me. Forever trying—and failing—until the end. Things looked bleak.

But I set those feelings aside and attended a church service, per Walter's suggestion, that Sunday.

The message I heard that serendipitous first visit was:

> *There is more life to be had. There is Power for Good in the Universe I can use to create a new life for myself.*

A spark of inspiration took hold in me that soon turned into a burning desire to learn everything I could about this new way of thinking. I was thrilled to finally have guidance that made sense. At last, some concrete direction—a path to run on.

Furthermore, I was now in the presence of dozens of loving beings who were also taking the steps necessary to get their lives back. Or better yet, to make way for something new. I was ready to take responsibility for my own life. *Yes*...all of it! *Yes*...I played a part in my own misery. And *yes*...it was up to me to change my approach if I wanted a different result. I know now what I didn't fully understand back then, that every time we take responsibility for our own life and our own actions, the energy of the whole world shifts toward greater love.

Something irrefutable took place that day. I don't even know what Kennedy Shultz, the man who would soon become my teacher, actually said. There was a different kind of communication going on. It went beyond words. There was an energy. He spoke from a place of spiritual authority with 'living' words, *life-giving* words, that touched me deeply.

I do know his message was ancient wisdom, from a time going back further than Jesus the Christ. There were ancestors of ours that knew much more about how to live in alignment with the Universe, understanding it as their life's purpose to be in balance and harmony with it. This was the kind of knowledge understood by great minds throughout history. As I became more familiar with these Universal Principles of Truth—Spiritual Laws—I practiced them. Like a madwoman, I applied them everywhere I could in my life. And sure enough, little by little, transformation took place. I'd found the Universal key.

I couldn't help but want to share my newfound insights with whomever would listen, including my kids. Now, in a welcomed addition to my role as their long-distance mother, I became their friend and practitioner. Together, we worked through the challenges they were facing.

At my day job, I even mentored a younger co-worker, Carol, who today I regard as a dear friend and sister. She had experienced enough by her early 20's to be ready for an empowering change in perspective. She listened to my testimony with intent, eager to jump in and create a new and improved life for herself, too! We became partners in this mutual quest.

One thing led to another, as it does. Manifestations of what I wanted to see happen started to appear. I had no idea where this was going, but I liked having an element of control over my life.

For the first time in a long time, life was moving in a positive direction. I was feeling more myself than I had in years, maybe ever. Of course, that is not to say I hadn't experienced positive upswings before, but something about this one was different. Before, things just kind of...happened, or didn't happen. Now, I was co-creating alongside the Universe, as a full and willing participant. I delved deeper into my studies and practice with the steadfast intention to master this process.

Was my life perfect from that point forward? No, of course not. It was quite messy, in fact. I had to give up on my idea of 'perfectionism'. A rigid concept like that can really keep you stuck. Soon after embarking on this journey, it became obvious that this untouchable standard I'd chosen to measure myself up against was going to have to go if I wanted to continue. I was going to have to trust in the infallibility of my Source, and let IT show me what could happen if I did. On this path, things would be changing constantly, morphing into something that had never existed before. If I was to live that life, I was going to have to get in shape to keep up!

In *Change Your Thoughts, Change Your Life*, Wayne Dyer writes, "The reality is that beginnings are often disguised as painful endings." Releasing the old makes way for the new. That is the way Life works. Like a caterpillar becoming a butterfly, just when we think our life is over, we learn how to fly.

CREATION, CREATION...THINGS FALLING APART, OTHER THINGS COMING TOGETHER, REARRANGING, ON AND ON...

That's the way it is! And that is exactly what happened. IT presented me with an endless buffet of options I'd never seen before – almost as if asking, "What about this? What about that?"

I would say, "yes," and it would continue to whip up increasingly more enticing demonstrations of what was possible. I was on my own private course with Life, custom-designed just for me.

We all want more. Even if we fear change, we still aspire to it, because we are infinite beings. We are alive in a system sustained by constant evolution. We are meant to evolve. We are meant to deepen, expand and thrive. We are meant to understand and master this life. There is something inside of us that knows how to do that. Embrace it! It is a beautiful thing! Follow the glimpses of your soul. Enter the new image in your mind's eye. Follow the impulses of your heart. These are your next steps!

Chapter Three: Inside Out World

"Nothing turns out different if I think about it in the same old way, because my thought, fresh ideas and a different perspective produces a new result out of an old situation. I change my life by changing my mind."

— Kennedy Shultz

"Give no power to the conditions of the world or the conditions of your life even though they are there because of us – stay focused on CREATION, just as God, Infinite Mind is, insist and persist on seeing things from the highest place and creating the greatest possibility."

— Emma Curtis Hopkins

To many of us, the world appears to be 'outside in'. Things outside of ourselves happen to us or around us. In Reality, our world is an 'inside out' one. This book is about learning to create whatever it is that you want and desire from the inside first. Changes must be made *behind the scenes*, before they can materialize on the outside.

It took me a long time to figure out that, as a person interacting with the world around me, I was limited in what I could do. I couldn't change the world. I couldn't get everyone to do what I wanted them to do. I had little to no control over what was happening around me. Trying to manage that which is outside yourself is like trying to manipulate a projection screen from the seats of the auditorium. To put in a new film, you need access to the control room. By the time I came to this realization, I had endured enough heartache, pain, and suffering to warrant a thorough search for a better way. Thankfully, there was one. And I was ready.

In the book *Dare, Dream, Do*, by Whitney Johnson (which I would recommend to anyone who has visions and great ideas, but hesitates to put themselves out there), there's a story of a young woman who is quite accomplished in her career, and has hopes of being a mother someday. When her first child arrives, she feels like she is failing miserably at it. She's tired, overworked, and not as present as she hoped she would be.

A noteworthy 13th century philosopher named Meister Eckhart penned the observation, "When the soul wishes to experience something, she throws an image of the experience out before her and enters into her own image." Meaning, the soul has far more authority than it lets the ego in on.

One day, a friend takes a picture of her and her son on a park bench. At first, she does what many of us do when we see a picture of ourselves: she criticizes her appearance. But upon closer observation, she notices something else. Through a different lens, she recognizes that she is a good mother. The picture hangs where she can see it, as a reminder to herself when she forgets. Her soul gave her a glimpse of what she was capable of, in a way that refuted all that she feared she was.

One of the biggest turning points in my life was making the shift from identifying as an employee of a demanding software company in Atlanta, where I couldn't go to the bathroom without it showing up on my time key, to identifying as an instrument of the Universe.

I was still working for that company, and still had all of my assigned roles and responsibilities, but that one idea...that *shift* in my thinking...brought about so many positive transformations in my life, not only for me but for those around me. Because of the shift in me, people approached me with their problems. I became a safe haven where they could open up. That was the real start of my work as a minister. It was the first time I realized how happy I was working first and foremost for the Universe, and not the Man! And ultimately, it was the first of many lessons in looking for the potential in any given situation, rather than just accepting things as they are.

A simple change in perspective opened the doorway to a whole new way of life. It allowed me to dedicate myself to a greater purpose and to an existence wherein I am always doing what I love. It's a realization that I am eternally grateful for. I'm not sure where I'd be today without it. I share my story, because I want everyone to know what is possible when we live in a more conscious and intentional way. Let these stories serve as a reminder that you are not powerless. We are beings of tremendous power, and we possess the ability to funnel that power into a co-creation process with no less than the Infinite, ITself.

How is that possible?

1. Prioritize (above all else) Soundness of the Self

Instead of structuring our lives around and *because of* the Outside World, by letting external factors and players determine who we think we are and how we choose to express ourselves, we can elect to pursue greater self-awareness by discovering our identity and cultivating a sense of self that flows from the inside-out. In a day-to-day sense, this practice implores us to make sure we're in a strong, good place (or rather 'God space') before any work in the outside world ever starts. For instance, *what kind of preparation do I need to do internally before I interact with others?* Even in the midst of conversation, when so many of us crack under the perceived pressure to respond quickly in spite of a lack of readiness to do so, there is no demand for urgency that outweighs the value of a grounded reply. Believe me when I say that others will be grateful to wait for you to get to a more loving, centered, collected place, as opposed to a combative or unsettled one.

2. Follow Your Heart, Not Your Head

Instead of trying to sort out what's best for you logically or intellectually, figure out what you actually *want* to be doing with your life. Listen to your inner guide, your inner Spirit, before anyone else. Allow yourself to be Spirit-driven in your actions and words. This practice requires that first: you must develop a strong relationship with and understanding of yourself in order to hear Spirit, loud and clear. Develop a partnership with the force behind and above life itself, meditate, be open to your infinite possibilities. Align yourself and your approach to life with the Infinite Intelligence that knows all. Let IT teach you and guide your hand. Resist the urge to unearth everything about the journey before you start. Follow the small steps you are given, and more will be revealed. Take time to dream about, visualize, and internally create what it is you hope to see. Discover your real intentions, and declare them. Make an effort to align yourself and your energy with that new vibration. Let the Universe work out the details.

Again, our universe is an inside out one. Our internal thoughts and feelings shape our world, and so if it is to be more to our liking, then we have to work in tandem with the Universe and its Laws. There can be no other way. The increasing complexity of the issues we continue to face today urges us to accept that we must work together, united by the higher power within us all, by whatever name we choose to call IT. Every time we shift to a greater idea, make a necessary adjustment in our thinking, course correct, we are aligned with our purpose, which brings us more joy and happiness.

Together we have reached a point in our consciousness evolution where enough people are choosing to think in a more positive and loving way that we are tipping the scales towards more goodness and well-being for us all. Isn't that exciting?

Everything we do as individuals affects the whole. Every time we change our thoughts, we change our world. It's up to us to think the highest, most loving, and most inclusive thoughts, because our thoughts determine the lens through which we see and interact with the world.

CONSCIOUSNESS EXPANDS...SPIRIT EXPANDS IN ITS EXPRESSION

AS US.

This is what we are here to do! The feeling that comes from living in alignment with your soul's highest purpose is as heavenly as it sounds.

Chapter Four: Home Is Where It All Comes Together

"To get out of this unending cycle, we have to allow ourselves to be drawn into sacred space, into liminality. All transformation takes place here. We have to allow ourselves to be drawn out of 'business as usual' and remain patiently on the 'threshold' (limen, in Latin) where we are betwixt and between the familiar and the completely unknown. There alone is our old world left behind, while we are not yet sure of the new existence. That's a good space where genuine newness can begin."

— Father Richard Rohr

There is so much to keep track of in today's world. With our increased intelligence and awareness comes greater complexity. Everything requires more of our attention, especially our ability to communicate and interact with one another. Even our finances have become complicated and difficult to manage. There's a lot more to them! We are bombarded with information.

Our homes are a very special places, our refuges from the world. Places where we go into our own little worlds, where our personal lives begin. The actual home, itself, no matter how big or small, needs to be in order. We need to have a place to go and be that makes sense; one that is comprehensively set up to support us and our lifestyle. Home includes our physical space, what that looks like, and how that space functions to optimally support healthy minds and bodies in active engagement with the world. Why is this so important? Our environment reflects our mental space. How clean, clear, and focused we are is reflected in our surroundings. Our homes also include our emotional space and how we feel when we are there.

Do we feel at home, at peace, at rest when we are home? When our home is a place of interpersonal conflict, limitations, or stress, the most vital part of our support system is in dysfunction. When we are happy being home, spending time with loved ones, having space to be ourselves, letting our hair down, so to speak, balance and harmony are restored.

Most of all, our home includes our spiritual space, a place that feeds our spirit. When we look around and see evidence of things that have meaning and are special to us, it helps us feel like we belong. A sweet friend gave me a rather large whale's tale, which I adore. Just like a whale diving deep, it reminds me to go deeper whenever I don't know what to do or things go awry. Home needs to be a place where we are free to meditate, play and express our creativity.

In *The Road Less Traveled,* Scott Peck describes the spiritual nature of a home in this way:

> *If one wants to climb mountains one must have a good base camp, a place where there is shelter and provisions, where one may receive nurture and rest before one ventures forth again to seek another summit. Successful mountain climbers know that they must spend at least as much time, if not more, in tending to their base camp as they actually do in climbing mountains, for their survival is dependent upon their seeing to it that their base camp is sturdily constructed and well stocked.*

Imagine yourself in a cabin at the base of a mountain. You are there to climb, and see all you can see. But above all, you are there to reach new heights. You want to know what you are made of. Any climb worth celebrating is sure to be a great test of strength, resilience and courage. For such a daunting feat, you'd be wise to prepare before you go. Your next steps may include taking a second (or third) look at the list of items you're carrying and the ones you're leaving behind, examining the condition of your gear, building up your mental and physical endurance, planning your route, and accounting for any possible mishaps along the way.

Overlooking even just one of these details could affect the success of the climb. Then, there's the mysterious element of timing—part of which can be estimated by probability, and part of which can only be measured by a clear intuition. On top of that, there are bound to be *other* climbers, one or more of whose plans may unexpectedly conflict with yours. It's a huge endeavor.

I have often thought of our home as a base camp, (or Santa's workshop with all the different projects we had going on). Through the years, that idea helped me to stay on track when the tedious attention to details got the better of me. There was a higher purpose involved: raising a child and doing work I loved. When there is a child involved, the goal is to get the child up and running and independent. Taking time to relax, play, and listen helps our children and partners with the fulfillment of their desires. This is key to each member making their own climb, whatever that is for them.

My hairdresser complimented my husband and me one day, remarking that we must've done a good job raising our son Joseph if he felt confident enough to go to college all the way across the country. It was nice to have someone recognize it as the success we considered it to be. Most others would half-(and only *half-*) jokingly remark something to the effect of "He couldn't get farther away from you, could he?"

To be fair, they weren't wrong. Orlando to Seattle—you really can't get much further apart without leaving the country. One family member was downright disturbed that we would ever "let him" go so far away. It's hard not to laugh when I think about it. Was there ever any stopping Joseph? And why would I ever want to stop someone from following their passion and chasing their dreams? Believe it or not, after spending almost 19 years under the roof of two strong-willed, passionately involved parents, he was more than ready to get out on his own and see what he could do. Even though John and I were clueless as to *how* this was going to happen, we were certain of his ability to find a way.

The summer before Joseph left for school felt like a triumphant descent, down from a mountain that had taken our family 18 years to climb. Now, it was time to prepare for the next. But on this one, Joseph would be climbing solo. He had already found his mountain. John and I would have to start searching for ours. It's important that everyone in the home participates in their own form of prep, climb, rest, repeat. We can get a kind of spiritual cabin fever if we stay at base camp for too long. Even as we age or lose mobility, the journey can always be tailored to fit our current range of motion.

All of this lends to the necessity of a sacred space, a place where we are nourished and fed—one we can share with those we care about. Successful living requires a lot of preparation. Many of us understandably get overwhelmed by the preparation stage and get stuck there. Preparing is the means to achieving the next iteration of who we came here to be. And while it is important, it is not the purpose of why we are here. It is far better to climb and die trying than to never set foot outside the door.

Scott Peck continues,

The ultimate goal of life remains the spiritual growth of the individual, the solitary journey to peaks that can be climbed only alone. Significant journeys cannot be accomplished without the nurture provided by a successful marriage or a successful society.

Spiritual communities are like base camps, too—groups of people working together to support one another in being more and living more meaningful lives. Ultimately, home is where the heart is. How we *feel inside* matters most. Having peace of mind and of heart are the most important aspects of being happy. Having a clear, focused mind and being happy attracts a peaceful, harmonious space we can call ours. Being happy also attracts the right people into our lives who are loving and supportive.

BASECAMP PREPARATIONS FOR ORDER AND ORGANIZATION

1. Determine what can be thrown out.

2. Recycle what can be recycled.

3. Gift unnecessary, but special, items to those who can appreciate them.

4. Donate whatever else you can.

5. Do whatever you can do now.

6. Affirm: My day is filled with Order and Organization.

Watch how you are guided to make the necessary changes. You intuitively know what needs to be released, to be given away—what you are done with. Celebrate however many steps you are able to take. You are heading in the right direction, and even the smallest amount of momentum can, and will, spiritually energize you to do more.

You will be given new ideas on how you can manage your personal business and career, how you can be more organized, how you can readily lay your hands on needed information, what systems you need to put in place to support your lifestyle and work. I found keeping a journal extremely helpful not only for writing out my "Ideal Days", but also for observations, realizations, demonstrations and things to appreciate. In the back of my journal, I write the name of a talk title or article I am working on, and every time something comes to me, I write it down. It makes it so much easier to have things in the same place. It is like putting a big pot of fresh, savory ingredients on the back burner to simmer, while you are doing other things. Let the Universe reveal what wants—or needs—to be shared. I am never disappointed by what ideas come forth. It's like a dance we do together.

This journal is very beneficial to me. Previously, I had notebooks and scraps of paper everywhere and it was difficult to keep track of them. This practice is one of many that keeps me centered and organized. From that place, I feel like I have a handle on things and can accomplish much more than I could before.

Whenever and whatever we invest in our physical surroundings is an investment in ourselves. Enough can't be said about how important our space is to our health and well-being.

Chapter Five: The Divine Setup

"The best and most beautiful things in the world cannot be seen or even touched – they must be felt with the heart."

— Helen Keller

"Your task is not to seek for love, but merely to seek and find all the barriers within yourself that you have built against it."

— Rumi

I haven't always appreciated my past and the players in my life, especially my family. The great thing about being around for a long time is getting to see the big picture. Perspective is everything. Now, I see how masterfully all has unfolded to support me in becoming all I came here to be. While once I felt unsupported, I now feel extremely and lovingly supported by all of life and everyone in it!

This chapter is an attempt to honor those who have been divinely placed to walk this path with me. I am so blessed.

A Moment of Gratitude For My Mom...

I had a dream about my mother that ultimately helped me appreciate her existence as more than just as one of my parents, more even than as a human being. I saw and felt her in pure Spirit so clearly; it is a meeting I will never forget. Three weeks after she passed, I dreamt that I was at a family gathering. She walked in from the back bedroom, and we locked eyes. She motioned at me to follow her. I asked her if she'd been sleeping. She said she'd been sleeping for a long time, and now she was awake. Her entire being radiated love and light. She held me close and looked into my eyes. The image of her pure joy and happiness was so powerful that I can still recall it lucidly as I write this. In that moment, I loved her, and she loved me, without restraint. We were one.

At once, I understood her genius, her frustrations, her coping mechanisms, her acceptance of me. I was not easy to live with as a teenager. I was a particularly rebellious type. Our family was religious, and I rejected all the beliefs imposed on me. I also rejected the stereotypical interests of women at the time, like cooking and homemaking. I openly questioned everything. And yet, she tolerated my dissent and differences of opinion, despite surely praying I'd take more after her in some areas. At that time, of course, I thought *she* was the one who was being difficult. I was blind to her positive qualities because I was fixated on the negatives. In reality, she was filled with so much beauty, warmth, and love.

The dream helped me to see how much I was like her, how much of her I have in me. She brought so much life to us all, even when we didn't understand or appreciate it. Her creativity with food, making a beautiful home for us to live in, making her own clothes for years so she could look good, even after having the five of us. She did whatever she could with what she had. And as busy as she was, she always had time to listen.

Thoughts of "What would Mom do?" seemed reasonably unavoidable as I approached my first dreary Christmas season away from home. Depressed and homesick, my attitude quickly changed as I considered my mother and all she did to make Christmas so very special every year. Thoughts of her inspired me to try to make the best of things and stop feeling sorry for myself. I immediately felt better. I took the money my parents sent us for Christmas and bought a small, artificial tree on sale from the drugstore, with a few days to spare. That helped set me in a new direction. That day I learned two valuable lessons: It was up to me to make the day special, and there is always something I can do to improve my situation. Thank you, Mom!

She absolutely spoiled us. We had dinner as a family almost every night of the year. We'd all gather at the table, bless our food, and enjoy a warm, full-course meal (always including desserts) that she'd prepared for us single-handedly while we swapped stories from the day.

During the holidays, her efforts were amplified with festive decorations, even *more* desserts, and hosting visits with our relatives throughout the season. She knew how to make things fun. She made every day special because she loved her family and our home.

She loved to read and write, but really she loved to learn. A natural mentor, she had a knack for relating her wisdom to others. Teaching at the Sunday School in her later years was just one of her many demonstrations of this.

Right after she graduated from high school, she joined a convent with a dream to become a nun. From there, she took an opportunity to work at the campus' pharmacy part-time while she continued to pursue her education in religious studies. After a year at the convent, she came to a conclusion that the life of a nun was not enough of the life she wanted. She wanted a family. And although she was adamant about her feelings of regret over not finishing school, she was being called to more. Shortly after leaving the convent, she met my father.

My parents had a beautiful love for each other. They met at Fort Leonard Wood, Missouri where Mom had helped serve meals to the troops. Now, she was called to live in the city of Milwaukee with my father's family and start a new life, and she said yes, despite the drastic change. Turns out I get my courage from her as well.

When she was in her 60's, after my father's passing, she was inspired to try her hand at writing for her church newsletter after reading some of the articles I wrote for our newsletter. She even left us with a beautiful journal that she created.

After she passed away, I was sorting through her belongings when I came across a thick stack of recipes she'd wanted to try. She loved the Food Network. As I've grown, the Food Network has become more enjoyable for me, too. I've found it to be nearly therapeutic to experiment with flavors and try new dishes. My mom continued to try to learn and share with others until the very end. It was a core part of her being.

It took a lot of living, and my own journey to mentorship, to fully understand the gifts she possessed. We shared a deep love that ultimately became a beautiful friendship. I owe much of who I am today to her, and to the (necessarily) challenging dynamic of our relationship. Thank you, Mom. I appreciate you more each day!

A Moment of Gratitude For My Dad...

It's taken me many years to fully accept and appreciate how much my father really loved me. I mistook his protectiveness for unwarranted limitation, thinking he was holding me back. In reality, I was blessed to have someone like him in my life to keep me from getting into too much trouble before I could fully understand the consequences. He and my mom both wanted the very best for their children, and worked hard to nurture the best within us all.

Dad was an industrious and hard-working man, always on-the-go. It's almost as if he knew he had less time and was determined not to waste it.

If my mother decided to take a rest during the day, he'd wonder out loud, "What are you saving yourself for?" If he noticed us kids staying inside, he begged, "Why aren't you taking advantage of this beautiful weather?" It's easy to see where my love of the outdoors comes from. When we were little, he'd round up all the kids in the neighborhood to go play ball at the schoolyard. He was also one of the few parents in the neighborhood who would initiate a game of soccer in the street without hesitation.

Aside from all he did for us at home, Dad spent thirty years fighting fires for the city of Milwaukee. He walked the line between traditional and modern man. A breadwinner who also cooked, cleaned, and changed diapers. But I suppose when you're a part of a big family, you learn how to pitch in.

He was the eleventh of twelve children. My paternal grandfather passed away before I had the chance to meet him, but my father's mother outlived both of her husbands. As she and his older siblings began to age, he readily stepped up to the plate as a caretaker. In my grandmother's final years, he continued to visit her regularly, resolved to ease her burden in any way he could. He operated from an ingrained sense of responsibility for those around him.

There is one memory in particular that I will never forget. I had just given birth to my daughter, and my parents came to visit us in Springfield, Illinois. Dad volunteered to watch a newborn Liz and a 3-year-old Nic so that Mom could take me out of the house for a breather.

My kids were breastfed and highly opposed to bottles, so we couldn't be gone for too long. When we got back, we found my father sitting in the rocking chair, facing the front window, with a screaming baby on one knee, and a talkative toddler on the other. Somehow, he had still managed to wash the kitchen floor and make a pot of soup.

Dad never went to college, but he possessed more practical skills than most. He learned how to do whatever it was that needed to be done, and that left him with a wide array of knowledge and talents. There wasn't anything he wouldn't try—wallpapering, tree-trimming, painting houses, and even learning how to play a small organ in our home. Nothing was off the table. He liked making meals for the firehouse, and the guys loved his cooking. He called home every night at 6, during his 24-hour shifts, to check in with my Mom. They would discuss their days and inevitably talk about new recipes for him to try.

Even in a lifestyle that seemed to be defined by hard work, he always made time for fun with his family. Whether it was playing golf, racquetball, or tennis with his brothers or planning day trips to the lake with us, he loved every part of life and led us by a strong example of how to live it to the fullest.

Both of my parents prioritized their relationship with God, making sure that all of us had a religious education through the 8th grade. They did their best to provide us all with the best model for life that they knew of: one centered on a connection to God. I didn't understand it at the time but, hopefully, as evidenced by the contents of this book, I do now.

He lived with relatively no health complications until in his early 50s, when he was badly injured in a fire. In fact, he actually *died* before being revived on the scene. He was in a coma, hospital-bound, until he was able to breathe without assistance, and then Mom brought him home to take care of him, assisted by a team of nurses. He remained in a coma for the last thirteen years of his life. For the first time, he was living in inaction. And for the first time in our lives, none of us—my siblings, aunts, uncles, grandma, mom, nor I—could count on his willingness to be there for us. Although we were all fully fledged adults prior to his injury, we were forced to grow up during those thirteen years in ways that we'd never had to before. He had been doing so much for everyone, all along, that when he no longer could, we had to find ways of doing more things for ourselves.

In return, we got to give back to him in ways that he'd never allowed us before. It was his time to receive—it was the only thing he could do. He stuck around long enough for us all to accept the fact that *this* was the way things were going to be from now on. Mom held out for the longest, but eventually, even she gave up on praying for her miracle and resigned to make the most of a life that was now just her own. I was blessed by each one of the twenty-eight (plus thirteen) years I got to spend with him.

A Moment of Gratitude For My Siblings...

I have been blessed with three younger brothers, Mike, Tom and Joe, and a sister, Nancy, who was the youngest. I wasn't always sure that having all of those brothers was a good thing, especially when it came to their pranks or disagreements, but had lots of fun times, too! Even so, when my mother was pregnant for the fifth time, I desperately prayed for a sister. This may have been the first time, in my rudimentary, insistent way, that I asked God for anything. My answered prayer was my first lesson on how to pray. Who knew the practice would serve me many years later as well? I was thrilled to have a beautiful sister come into my world!

I can't thank enough my siblings and all of their wonderful spouses—who have become siblings too over the past 40 years. Each one of them has unique gifts they have shared with me that touch me deeply. I love them all. Even though they have not always understood me, they have been loving and supportive throughout my entire life. Today we enjoy precious time together and celebrate the beautiful families we have created.

A Moment of Gratitude For Colette...

We met close to sixty years ago, when I was ten. I was the new kid on the block when we moved, and in need of a friend. I made some connections at my school, and there were two other girls on my street, but Colette and I were immediately close. We bonded over a shared love of nature, reading, and the show *Dark Shadows,* of all things! Even after we moved away, grew up, and could no longer see each other in person as often as we once did (due to the busyness and bustle of our independent lives), our bond has remained sturdy throughout nearly sixty trips around the sun. I only remember once our lives seemed to be drifting apart due to the demands of our everyday life. I will never forget her saying: "I am not giving up on this relationship. It is too important to me. I want you in my life." She has been with me through thick and thin and has remained by my side through my darkest times.

One year, she and her husband had planned a trip to Orlando, where John and I were living at the time. We were scheduled to be out of town for a conference, so I invited her and her family to stay at our house. Before we left, I spent several hours cleaning and preparing the space, wanting to make it feel as comfortable and welcoming for them as I could. She fondly reminisces on the fact that I left chocolates on their pillows, just like a hotel. Since her retirement, we've been able to call and visit each other more frequently. I will cherish her always. She was a gift from the Divine.

A Moment of Gratitude For Cynder...

What a breath of fresh air! On the heels of my first marriage, and on a temporary hiatus from college, I was a 21-year-old living in a small conservative town just outside of Milwaukee. Life got serious in a heartbeat. My then-husband was a police officer and his working hours were all-consuming and erratic. I quickly learned that marriage wasn't the final destination I'd believed it to be. There was still a need every day to find something meaningful to do with my time. On a walk around the small downtown area one day, I wandered into a social agency in search of a job, and there she was. Even though there wasn't a job opening, Cynder and I hit it off right away, and I walked back home feeling accomplished. What a delightful friend she became! She was well-versed in new and old spiritual literature, always recommending something for me to read. One of these recommendations introduced me to the work of Joseph Campbell, an expert in comparative mythology and religion who wrote *The Power of Myth*, among other books. She saved me from a lifetime of boredom and lack of direction. She has held a special place in my heart for the past fifty years.

A Moment of Gratitude For Nic & Liz...

Nic and Liz are my beloved eldest children. You can be sure to hear more about their unmatched strength, beauty, and magnificence in the chapters to come. Nic was our Christmas present in 1978, and Liz was our Easter baby in 1982. I talked to them like they were adults from the very beginning, aware that although their minds were new, they were also fresh from the other side of the veil. When Nic was a toddler, he and I would talk about Mother Nature, which was my personification of God at the time. I reminded Liz often that she was beautiful on the inside and out. Somehow, I knew they were so much more than they appeared to be. How could they not be? I couldn't look into those deep ocean-blue eyes without seeing God, feeling the connection. Fresh from Spirit, newly created beings. I was in awe of their purity and greatness.

I learned early on that they were my teachers, too. They both came into the picture before I knew how to consciously create. Their presence pushed me to re-evaluate the things within myself that, up until then, I'd just accepted as a part of my reality. That is one of the hardest-hitting truths one can face as a parent.

My biggest regret was that I was not able to give them what they needed. I wasn't always there for them. When my father fell into a coma, all I could think about was being with him. We lived roughly five hours apart, and it tore me apart to not be there for him. It seemed wholly impossible to be there for everyone in the way that they needed me to be, all at the same time. I didn't have anything left to give. Any direction I looked in seemed like the wrong one. I was devastated. The stress on my marriage was overwhelming and more than young people in their 20s are equipped to handle. My internal state declined further than I'd previously known to be possible.

Contemplating whether or not my clearest path to recovery involved me leaving my children was a spiritual low I wouldn't wish on anyone. Marlo Morgan, a dear friend and author, tried her best to reframe my shame with the perspective that, "You went ahead to find the way for your children." Those words have stayed with me throughout the decades of motherhood, and over time I have allowed myself to accept them more and more. I had to rebuild myself in order to be there for them, in all of the ways I wish I could've been there from the start.

My path partner, Carol, echoed these words in a similar sentiment years later: "You never left your children." Despite the physical space between us, I always carried them with me. As I learned new insights about myself and the Universe, they were always the first on my list of people to share them with. Together, we are creating a life we never could've had. It was Liz who said, "I have enough love in my heart for four parents," when her father remarried.

A Moment of Gratitude For Cousin Walter...

As you know, Walter is the saving grace that I was fortunate enough to be related to. Without his guidance, I can't be sure what path I would've ended up on in the wake of my life's fallout almost forty years ago. Despite our interactions being nearly exclusive to the trips to visit my mother's family in St. Louis, he graciously welcomed me with open arms in my time of need.

He knew exactly what I needed—a connection to my own spirituality. He got me back to church. He'd found something he loved, and willingly shared it with me: Science of Mind. Through his own demonstrations, he showed me what a life could look like. That was the beginning of a bright future that exceeded anything I could've imagined was possible for myself at that time. It was also the beginning of a long-overdue solidifying of my friendship with this strong, unique spirit. An added benefit to going back to church was opening me up to the community of individuals who later became some of my closest friends.

He was a professor of Special Education at Georgia Southern, where he was well loved for his creativity in making things interesting for his students, and he retained a passion for learning well past his time in school. There was *no one* I could relate to like him! His objective, gentle encouragement and guidance were exactly what I needed to be able to heal and begin again.

Who could've guessed that a formerly distant older cousin of mine would play such a vital role in my life's journey? This relationship appears to have been 'set up' for us both from the very beginning.

A Moment of Gratitude For Ken...

Walter paved the path that led me to Dr. Kennedy Shultz, the minister of the Atlanta Church for Spiritual Living. From the first talk I had the pleasure of attending, I knew I was where I was meant to be. He is one of the few people in this world I would gladly listen to forever. In the wake of my dad's passing, he became a father figure to me. They were similar in the aspects that mattered.

My father was firm in his faith, and Ken was consistent in his. First and foremost, they were men of character. Both had a great desire to share and support those around them.

When I was a teenager, Dad would quietly drop off religious excerpts and snippets of advice from Ann Landers on the top of my bedroom dresser. I wasn't really open to life advice at the time, especially from my conservative parents. Fast forward to now, after significant time in the trenches we often find ourselves in, my tune has changed. I was open to learning all I could from this timeless teaching—from the Wisdom of the Ages. Now I'm the one sending my unassuming offspring bits and pieces of it.

Some don't ever get to experience a positive male role model in their lifetime. I was blessed with two who just gracefully fell into place one after another.

From my first visit to the church, I was certain that there was much to learn from Ken. He was a steady voice of reason to trust in, while I was rebuilding trust with my own voice. He was a gifted man, who'd seen his way through a slew of personal difficulties and chose to share his wisdom from experience with others. Ken's talks were bright, uplifting and inspirational. They resonated with my entire being. He masterfully combined personal anecdotes and familiar themes in our world's history with kernels of the Universal Truth in a way that opened up our consciousness to a greater understanding and appreciation of life. He was a father, a friend, and a mentor, all in one. He presided over many important moments in my life, eventually marrying me to John, hosting a welcoming ceremony for Joseph, and ordaining me as minister.

His teachings helped us embody better versions of ourselves in the world. They didn't make us want to get off the grid and live in a hut in the middle of the forest so we could better focus on God; instead, they taught us how to maintain a two-way connection with God in any situation we might encounter throughout our everyday lives.

I will always remember one seemingly specific and practical common courtesy he brought to our attention: *Don't stiff the waiter.* By this he meant we should make our disappointments known to the establishment, or the one in charge of it, early on. It's not right to punish the one who serves. Of course, this wisdom is applicable to more than just Sunday brunch. Another wise phrase he often said: *One's dollars can go places we will never go.* Giving financially to the world gives us some ownership in it. This idea expanded my view of myself and what I could do.

More and more, I've come to know that 'growing up' involves much more than what any one or two parents can give us. It involves a lifetime of hands-on experience, evaluation, and conscious observation of the world around us, and within us, in order to get to a strong, centered place with ourselves.

By the time I met Ken, it had become crystal clear to me that I could not trust myself. This new understanding was perhaps most poignantly evidenced by the huge mess I'd made of my life by the start of my thirtieth year. In my early twenties, I thought I knew everything. Now, it was back to ground zero.

I had to admit I didn't know at all what I was doing *out there* in the world. It is a blessing that I was presented with little other choice but to acknowledge this. It opened me up to accepting the assistance and guidance of others. My only role was to train myself to recognize what guidance was right for me to follow, rather than reinventing the wheel (so to speak). When I look back today, something inside of me *did* know what I needed, and it knew how to get me there.

Now that I was willing to take a step back, out of my own way, I could see that nothing else was ever going to stop me.

When one crab tries to escape from a bucket, the others instinctively pull it back in in their own effort to try and get out. Before Ken's teachings, I was clearly a crab in a bucket—frustrated and powerless because of the perceived helplessness of my apparent situation. With every day, my chances of survival seemed to be getting slimmer. Few ever make that great escape. I was fortunate enough to be open enough to allow such an opportunity to present itself, and to be determined enough to give it everything that I had.

A Moment of Gratitude For Carol...

Talk about just the right person showing up at just the right time! This beautiful soul welcomed me into her life as if I was a long-lost sister.

She started working in the accounting department of a well-known building supply company in Atlanta a few months after I did. Suddenly, my dreary, smoke-filled temp-job environment was transformed into an inviting and lively one. For whatever reason, some of the most beautiful souls in this world have been through some of life's harshest experiences. She saw in me what I saw in her: a weathered heart ready for more. She was one of the first people I had the opportunity to share my new perspective with; one of my first opportunities to return the favor and experience the truth from the otherside of the table. It was self-assuring to see how easy it was for me to offer her support and encouragement. We became fast friends. Anything I could do was better with her: we walked together, we ran together, we went to classes together.

She and I spent hours discussing these time-honored spiritual principles as we learned more about them together, and we became proficient in writing mind treatments about what we each wanted to experience for ourselves. We were both co-creating for the first time in our lives. As a newbie, this was an exciting experience on its own, but it was a blessing to be able to do it with such a cherished friend.

Despite our nine-year age difference, Carol and I had no problem accepting each other as the in-progress individuals that we were. She understood me and extended an appreciation for me in a way that no one had before. We've remained a team on this spiritual adventure for over thirty-five years. Thank you, Carol, for all of the encouragement and love you've selflessly given over these years. You are most definitely a blessing—a soul I was destined to find along my best path!

A Moment of Gratitude For Ray...

Soon after becoming a minister, I started up a metaphysical discussion group at our local bookstore in an effort to extend the reach of our community. I was fortunate to have met so many wonderful people throughout my time in the group, a good handful of which are still in my life today. My dear friend Ray was one of them. She is no longer with us, but will remain in my heart forever. Her son introduced her to the group, and from then on, she continued to join us for our services every Sunday morning until her passing.

During the first month or so of her attendance, she approached me after a meeting one day with a message: "You need help."

She went on.

"Tell you what. You do what you do best: teach, lead, and talk. I will take care of the business side of things."

I didn't know what to say. I was floored...in a good way. There was no question that I needed help. Building and maintaining a spiritual community is no easy task. I trusted her, and I gladly accepted her offer.

Over the course of our business partnership, we developed an equally close friendship that extended beyond our work together—so close that she was the first call we made the morning of Joseph's birth. She and I were inseparable and in sync with our plans and our visions at work. We enjoyed this dynamic for over six years. She helped to set the stage for me to take my relationship with God to another level. Because of her, I knew what it was to be unconditionally loved, understood, and supported.

At the end of our time together, Ray had completed her coursework and was newly installed as a minister. Just one year later, she made her transition to the other side. She'd struggled with health problems almost all of her life, starting in her teenage years when she was put on steroids for her chronic pain. She remained on them for much of her adult life until her body finally gave way. Her passing was a loss felt by the entire community. Ray earned her Reverend title long before she got it. She was a gift I didn't know I needed.

My time with her was a perfectly orchestrated segue into my own everlasting partnership with God. Her death emphasized even further what I had been resisting: the need to go inside and develop my own true and personal connection with Spirit.

A Moment of Gratitude For Sam...

When Ken, our teacher, encountered a health challenge, Sam, Chris (other offspring ministers of Ken's), and I began doing mind treatments together for him. We continued our group work for some time until Chris was called to move in another direction. Sam and I continued on, and over the course of our next twenty-five years of treatment work, he became a confessor of sorts, someone to share my deepest secrets with. We continue to work together regularly to listen, to be there for each other and to know the greatest possible outcomes to whatever is going on. It has been an honor and privilege to know him. He is a phenomenal listener, calls things as they are, tells me what I need to hear, and truly knows and understands Consciousness. It's no wonder that he gives some of the most amazing mind treatments I've ever received. He has become a dear friend. If only everyone could have a Sam.

A Moment of Gratitude For Fred...

Sometime within the first five years of my ministry, I received a letter from a prisoner who'd found out about my work through a Creative Thought magazine put out by our organization. Inside the letter was a picture of a young Caucasian man.

He admitted to me that he had not finished high school, and he often apologized for his imperfect literacy. Although his vocabulary was often simple, his mind and his heart were not. His loving spirit took in the words of truth I shared with him. Whatever he resonated with, he shared with the inmates around him and even back again to me.

Early on, we started sending him relevant literature and stationery, so that he could have greater contact with the outside world. He found his place on our regular list of recipients during Christmas time, and of course on his birthday. He would write back thanking us for the opportunity to share the highest quality food the prison offered, cheeseburgers, with his fellow inmates. One cannot live on bread alone. Love and connection are of the highest nutrition to the soul, and he was empowered through an ability to give back to those around him.

He had so much to share with the world, and given his circumstance, I was fortunate to have been one of the people who received his gifts. The positivity he manages to radiate through his letters, in the midst of so many difficult situations—which he rarely delves into—often gives me the impetus to 'keep on keeping on' in my own life.

It wasn't until years later that he revealed an unexpected truth to me that he'd felt a need to withhold. He did this with another picture of himself. This time, it was of his true appearance. He was a beautiful African American man. Having been judged and rejected by countless people in his life, including his own family, for selling drugs, he was cautious about what he could share about his true self. At the start of our communication, he feared that someone might disregard his words because of the color of his skin. I responded in order to assure him that his ethnicity had no bearing on my respect or care for him. I knew his true identity: God.

"I am doing great. I see love and joy in everyone I see and I pray that they can see it in themselves. More Good things are to come for us ALL. Love, Fred."

Even now, it's hard to say who is there for whom. I am grateful to know him as an integral part of my life. He is a gift of grace that continues to give. Almost three decades later, he's never stopped taking the time out of his days to craft inspirational messages for me, and he continues to encourage my work in the ministry.

***

There are other beautiful souls that have been a part of the divine plan for me as well. Molly, a school administrator and career counselor, helped me plan my next steps. She got me into some technical classes that would help me get a better paying job. She became a dear friend, taking me on walks, listening to me process and making helpful suggestions. She was later responsible for my decision to train to run in the annual Peachtree Road Races in Atlanta.

A letter came out of the blue from Dr. Michael, a life-long prisoner who had been part of an unfortunate situation in his late teens. An avid writer and student, he grabbed onto the Science of Mind teachings by Ernest Holmes. I asked him to write the forward to my second book, *Energize Your Creative Super Powers*. He went on to co-author a book, *My Search for Ancient Wisdom: One Prisoner's Journey of Transformation*.

I can't possibly mention all of the incredible people who have touched my life. Many new ones come into the picture anytime I begin collaborating with the Universe on a new project. All help to inform my next steps forward. When I look back at the path I've walked to get to where I am today, I see the intersections of all of these individuals' paths with my own, and how these connections were destined, and Divinely Planned. Some of our paths run parallel, others cross only now and again, some only once.

I am blessed to have found a way to walk through life where whenever I am in need there is another traveler on the way to help reassure me of the best way forward, to hold my hand, to love me, and help me traverse the patches of rough terrain. I can't help but feel an overwhelming sense of gratitude for their roles in my journey. They are all gifts of God that appeared unbidden, and all exemplify grace.

Chapter Six: Spiritual Tools

"The highest attitude of mind, from which all else springs, is one of perfect calm and absolute trust in the Spirit. The one who can with perfect confidence look into the future and with perfect ease of mind rest in the present, and who never looks backward, but who has learned to be still in his own soul and wait upon the Spirit, he is the one who will the most completely demonstrate the supremacy of spiritual thought over all so-called material resistance. Be still and know that I AM God."

— Ernest Holmes, *Creative Mind*

Spirituality is more than a belief system, it is a way of life. It requires a tangible application to our day-to-day choices and actions if it is to become all that it can be. It is entirely possible to implement spiritual tools into every arena of our lives: relationships, work, finances, health, education, self-care. When we do, existence takes an interesting turn for the better. Undeniable results that we never could have conceived of start showing up. This chapter includes the central methods of practice that I use to achieve my desired results. While this is by no means an exhaustive list, these are some of my favorites.

In order to provide a more comprehensive understanding of my work *behind the scenes*, I have included both the name and a brief description of each one of the tools I've used to demonstrate the blessings I've included in this book. My hope in doing this is that an understanding of the process of using them, in combination with my examples of their real-life application and efficacy, will help you decide to transform your own life for the better. For an even deeper explanation of the concepts I've listed, please refer to my workbook, *Energize Your Creative Super Powers, 7 Ways to Spiritual Fitness*.

Spiritual Tool: Affirmation

Our words have power—both in the world and within our own spirit. One or two lines declaring what you know to be true (or more often what you *want* to know to be true) can turn your thinking around in an instant. Affirmations are essentially like mantras. You recite them whenever you find yourself caught up in a negative mindset about yourself, your circumstance, or your world. They are a quick pick-me-up—a reminder of the greater truth around you. A well-crafted affirmation works to quickly realign our focus and shift our mental energy back to grounded truth and love. This naturally leads to improved conditions and, if nothing else, *feeling better* in the face of a struggle. For example:

I am surrounded by and immersed in love.

Spiritual Tool: Intention

Before you start your day, ask yourself, *what is my intention?* This can be an overall intention for the day or one that is specific to an important event, task or goal. *What is my intention for this call? What would I like to have happen in this meeting?* Throughout Joseph's childhood, we'd ask him every morning, "What kind of day are you going to have?" Most of the time, especially when he was younger, he'd respond somewhere along the lines of, "A fun one." It can be that simple. The act of defining your intention before your action, whatever it may be, gets your mind and body on the same page. You don't even necessarily have to repeat the intention once you've set it (although it certainly can help), because your thoughts, words, and actions will hold onto whatever intention you've set and respond accordingly.

We project unconsciously all the time without giving it a thought. We haven't a clue that we are the creators of our experiences or at least of our part in them. We have a part in the creation of everything that involves us. We go into our days ready to brave whatever we happen to face without having a clue that our presence, our conscious awareness of what we would like to see happen could make a tremendous difference. If we go into a day or a meeting or appointment with dread or fear, unsure of ourselves, the outcome could be less than what we would like to experience. Setting a general intention of what could be best, instead of living as reactors to life, empowers us to live from a high-minded place. By taking time to really think about what we *truly* want—what is in everyone's highest and best interest—we can override the often negative side effects of letting our instinctual and unconscious intentions run the show.

Ask yourself, *how do I want to feel during the process?* How do you want to feel in the end? Instead of assuming things are going to go well on their own, essentially flying blind into the realm of possibility and averages (like a coin flip—you win some, you lose some), put yourself in the driver's seat. Your odds of success are sure to increase if you're well-prepared. Acting from an assured, open, loving place yields far better results than not. Setting a clear, conscious intention aligns you much more closely with the Law of Attraction that *out-pictures* all outcomes. This practice puts you in a co-creative role with the Universe, instead of a passive, reactionary one. The results speak for themselves.

Spiritual Tool: Meditation

This tool involves a practice of stilling the mind and body in a manner that allows you to receive the messages of the Universe without obstruction or confusion. The Universe is communicating with us all the time, but do we as a people always know how to interpret and understand what's being said? Those who don't may only know continuous conversation, mental clutter, noise. There is no empty space for the Divine to get a clear message through over all of the speech, thoughts, music, television, and other distractions. Some people in our world do not yet know the joyful experience of being at enough peace with themselves to be comfortable in silence.

For the vast majority of my early life, it felt nearly impossible to sit still long enough to meditate. When I became privy to the other forms this practice can take, outside of the classic sit-on-a-pillow-with-your-eyes-closed-and-do-nothing, I gained some traction. *Walking meditation* was an acceptable place for me to start. You have to meet your spirit where you're at. For beginners, classic meditation is often an overextension. It certainly was for me. To this day, nothing compares to taking a stroll out in nature, and allowing it to fill me up with its energy. Besides its practicality as a spiritual tool, it keeps me active, and allows my mind to freely wander while still keeping it centered on the simple truths. Alfred Tennyson, a poet that often mused about metaphysics and the relationship between humankind and nature during the mid-to-late 1800s, famously wrote in his poem "Flower in the Crannied Wall":

> *"Little flower—but if I could understand,*
> *What you are, root and all, and all in all,*
> *I should know what God and man is."*

My walks are for the purpose of surrounding myself in nature, listening to it, and getting back into alignment with my Source. It is in this state, in whatever way you manage to achieve it, that our mind can open up to Divine ideas and perspectives.

Over the years of my practice, it has become easier to sit and be still. The ability to practice meditation within the body, as well as in the mind, is where the real magic happens. When we do, resistance of every kind falls away. Life-changing insights just *happen*. We come to understand, not just in logical spiritual sense, but to our core, that there is less for us to do and more for us to *be*. It's hard to believe that we can accomplish as much as we can, sitting in the comfort of our favorite chair. But that's just it. Life doesn't *have* to be uncomfortable. We don't have to break our backs to achieve success or to be worthy of bliss. Our Spirit does all of the heavy lifting. As time passes, and your practice deepens, you will begin to notice the subtle, quiet shifts that are positioned to move mountains in your life. And eventually, there will come a point when you can't imagine your world without this precious meditative time.

Spiritual Tool: Visualization

This tool is particularly fun, because it exercises the imagination. It is the act of stretching your mind to be open to the *ever more* of what's possible—of setting aside a few minutes to fantasize, daydream, or even pretend what your life could be or what a particular area of it might look like, in your mind's eye. Visualize your dreams coming true. Visualize yourself living in the perfectly constructed picture, and spend some time there, before it's ever realized in the material reality. If you can't quite come up with a clear image of what you want, start by identifying any feeling of lack that you find yourself returning to and go from there. What feeling, the opposite of that feeling of lack, would you like to experience? Imagination is a key muscle in the act of co-creation. It needs to be strong and flexible. This can be achieved through an exercise like visualization.

Spiritual Tool: Visioning

Visioning is another way to connect us to our Higher Power. It sounds similar to Visualizing but it is different. This tool involves a specific process that positions us in a way that's different from how we are generally accustomed to working.

I use this tool when I'm seeking Divine advice on what to do, or where to go, next. The Universe's omniscient, omnipotent, omnipresent Intelligence knows more about everything and everyone than *anyone* else, so it's a pretty great resource.

In visioning, we put forth our questions and listen. *I am open to the highest wisdom that would like to happen*. We are seeking a picture, similar to visualization. But in this practice, we are not putting out a specific image as our ideal. Our only desire is to have an idea revealed to us that is *greater* than any we can imagine on our own. We are allowing the ideal image to come to us. We may have a need to fulfill, but have no clue how to achieve it, or aren't even sure what the best outcome for our situation would be. This tool helps us embody a deeper receptivity within ourselves so that we may gain clarity to that which is still vague.

Specifically, we are seeking an answer to the following questions in relation to whatever desire we are directing them to:

- What does Spirit want to experience through us in the realm of our... (expression, path, relationships, physical location, health, wealth, career)?
- How does that look and feel?
- What strengths do I bring to the situation?
- What can I release to make room for this to come about?
- What do I need to embrace?
- Is there anything else I need to know?

This practice may bring instant results—or not. Sometimes inspirations, solutions, and ideas come days or even weeks later. As you continue to work with this tool, you will learn to appreciate and recognize the subtle and often unexpected ways positive change can take place.

This method was developed by Dr. Michael Beckwith, a founder of the Agape International Spiritual Center in Los Angeles. More about this tool can be found in his work online, as well as in my workbook *Energize Your Creative Super Powers*.

Spiritual Tool: OMG!s

This is another great tool for exercising the imagination muscle. It is a method of stepping into the reality of what you'd like to have happen before it does. You project yourself to a future date, by which it has all played out. Then, you describe how wonderful that reality is, looking back from the future in which you've achieved it. This practice can be credited to Mary Morrissey, as featured in her *Prosperity Plus Program,* where she details the process of sharing a verbal recollection of how you achieved a desired goal with a practice partner. They are called OMG!s because, in best practice, they contain verbiage that communicates an energy of *oh my God! I have to tell you what happened...*

In my own practice, I prefer to write the experience down on an index card, large or small depending on how descriptive I feel like being. Write today's date in the top right corner, and underneath it, write the date you'd like to have the experience you are describing. Within the lines, describe the event as if you are talking to a friend who hasn't yet heard the news. Let yourself feel the success of achieving the goal as you write. Let it come through your words, but don't get hung up on the practical details of step one, step two, step three. The Universe responds to feeling, and as such, it is far more important to embody the kinds of feelings we wish to experience than it is to try and determine a concrete plan of how those feelings should come about. Remember, Spirit will take care of that part.

An OMG! about a desired move might go something like this...

Oh my God! I have to tell you what happened. John and I discovered the absolutely perfect place to land and live! We are thrilled at how many ways it suits us and our lifestyle. It serves our family beautifully. It is a gorgeous setting that feeds us and fills us up tremendously. Our infinite wealth totally supports us living this way. It feels delightful to have found such a beautiful place that brings us comfort and joy. It feels more like home than any other place has ever felt because we are at home with ourselves now in a way in which we weren't before. We are overwhelmingly happy! Thank you, Universe!

Notice how I did not detail a particular town or home. Another reason I recommend steering clear of such descriptors is to keep the door open to possibilities we're not yet aware of, and ones that are better than any we currently know about. I use this technique often when I need to boost my own believability and confidence in the end result. Sometimes, even the act of writing the successful feelings down on paper will bring up new solutions and perspectives. Come back to the card often and each time allow yourself to feel again the energies it elicits. It's exciting to see what transpires as you go, and to have something to look back on once it becomes your reality.

SPIRITUAL TOOL: *Ideal Days*

This is probably one of my most-used spiritual tools. It's particularly useful for getting a grip on an extremely demanding list of to-dos and responsibilities. I first learned about it in a Mastery Class I attended several years into my ministry taught by my husband, John. Essentially, it's the practice of writing down what an ideal day would look like. I've created a more structured format to make it even easier to use on a daily basis.

Not everyone believes that there even is such a thing as an ideal day, but I invite you to try out the process for yourself. Every morning you write the essence of what you would like to experience for that day. You could do it the night before going to bed depending on your focus and energy at that time. You want to give this exercise your best time and energy because this will literally help you to create the kind of day you want to experience, the kind of relationships you want to have, the kind of work you want to do, the experience you want of yourself, and how you want to feel through it all. This is an expansion of the practice of setting your *Intention* for what you would like to see happen. This helps you zero in on the main focus for your day. This is an opportunity to get into the consciousness of your desire and do behind-the-scenes work.

Emma Curtis Hopkins, a powerful teacher of the early 20th century, said it this way: "Every day, take time to sit and write. Name your good." Why? Because our thoughts are creative. It's like we are broadcasting a signal, and that signal must manifest in physical form and experience. This is a great way to co-create with the Universe and live every day to the fullest. I have used this practice for almost 20 years now, and it continues to make a huge difference in my life. It helps me to remember that I am a powerful creator. When I stay in creation, I actively see my interplay with Life throughout the day. This daily rhythm builds as I continue, and it supports me in being all I can be, enjoying the creation of the beautiful garden of life.

A full-page copy of this exercise can be found in the Addendum for an example or a place to start.

Spiritual Tool: Mind Treatment

Spiritual Mind Treatment is a proven tool for shifting consciousness designed by Ernest Holmes, founder of Science of Mind, after all of his studies of world religions, teachings, philosophies and personal experience.

Mind Treatment is really a form of prayer—often called affirmative prayer because it is made up of definite, positive statements of Truth. It is not begging, bargaining or beseeching with a distant deity who needs convincing and only comes around every now and then to check on us. Rather it is recognizing that God is *ALL* there is. There is nothing else. There is no other Power in the Universe. We are one with our Source. IT is here to support us and wants us to succeed. IT continuously provides for us as IT does for all ITs creations.

This is a tool to shift consciousness out of the obvious condition into the spiritual realm of Truth. It's called treatment because it treats our minds. It gets our thoughts into alignment with the Universal Mind or Spirit.

This is an active, alive, conscious communication with the Beloved. It's not talking to an intangible entity, completely separate from *ourselves*. It goes beyond prayer as we formerly knew it. It is not passive like meditation where we get quiet and listen. Some call it a prayer treatment to signify that it is still very much a prayer—a more evolved form of prayer—one that engages us in an active, ongoing participation with Life. As we relate to the Infinite Intelligence of the Universe, we begin to yield extraordinary results. Everything becomes more exciting. We quickly see that living this way is the main event in terms of the human experience.

Five to seven steps are generally used to make up a full Mind Treatment. I teach seven. You can use less. It's helpful to be familiar with them all, as different circumstances require more.

THE SEVEN STEPS OF MIND TREATMENT

Recognize a higher power.

Remind yourself that you are ONE with IT.

Embody the idea you are creating (of health, wholeness, perfection, abundance, whatever it is).

See what happens to be in your way and release it. Recognize any fear, doubt or sense of giving up your power in a situation, and release it: "I release my doubts about this happening now. I just let them go."

More strongly than ever, affirm what you know to be your real truth about the situation.

Give thanks.

"I am complete. And so it is!"

A full-page copy of this exercise can be found in the Addendum for an example or a place to start.

There are many tools available through which to open our minds and hearts. The best ones are those that speak to us. Those are ones we can get behind and commit to using. That doesn't mean the same ones have to be used all the time. It is helpful to have a handful of practices that will come in handy for different scenarios. I go to whichever one speaks to me at the time.

Rarely do I use just one method for something that is important for me. It's usually a combination which keeps me interested until the result is achieved. In these writings, contemplation mostly took place on my walks in nature, or sometimes, while doing the dishes. Nature, especially, is the perfect place to fill us up with its energy, let our thoughts wander, invite and entertain innovative solutions, and think never-before thoughts.

With so much nature in Central Florida, I had plenty of opportunities to enjoy the different wildlife that showed up each time I went out. The animals always represented some sign or meaningful message that I needed to get. Hence, animal totems became a large part of my spiritual practice. They were my connection to the otherworldly—to Spirit. The pages of my journals are filled with more thrilling encounters than I can mention. Journaling dreams is still a part of my daily work, as well. Dreams are good indicators of what is going on in our subconscious. Numbers showing up in our dreams or in our awake time have significant meanings and messages, too. The practice of interpreting dreams and numbers varies from person to person, so I chose not to include my own interpretations.

The practices I like the most are the ones listed here. Setting an *Intention* is always a great place to start. It sets the mood for what we would like to see happen. When I want to create, I use *Ideal Days* and the *OMG!* cards. When I really need to make strong, powerful shifts, I go back to basics and use *Mind Treatments*. They help me get my mind straight by aligning with Universal Truth. *Meditation* plays a larger role in my everyday experience than ever before. I love the subtle shifts it gives me throughout my day, helping me to see things differently and giving me answers. I go to *Visioning* when I have no idea where to start. It stokes the fire and gets things going. I continue to use everything as part of my practice, including in my marriage. It takes regular practice to have a healthy, loving relationship. All of these are constant reminders that help me stay on track and protect me from the rabbit holes life tries to send me down.

These practices have been proven to work, and with a little dedication, they will work for you, too. I invite you to experiment with these, allow them to change as you go, and even create your own. Be creative and open yourself up to the new. Look at the practices that energize your spirit and focus on those. There are no hard-and-fast rules here. The purpose of these tools is to grow us, to expand the way we think, get us into alignment with Spirit and open ourselves up to the Divine Universal God Mind that knows all and gives us access to unlimited Intelligence.

Section II consists of significant demonstrations I have experienced up until now and examples of the Behind-the-Scenes work I did to accomplish them. There is much Behind-the-Scenes work that I don't have a record of, but I believe there is plenty here to give you an idea of how this works.

Section II

The Show

Chapter Seven: John

"The most beautiful people we have known are those who have known defeat, known suffering, known struggle, known loss, and have found their way out of the depths.

These persons have an appreciation, a sensitivity, and an understanding of life that fills them with compassion, gentleness, and a deep loving concern. Beautiful people do not just happen."

— Elisabeth Kübler-Ross

It was clear that I needed a break from relationships with men. Wonderful as they are, I knew that I had to take time to mend my relationship with myself before I could reasonably expect to build a bond with someone else. One of the silver linings to the end of my first marriage was an opportunity to put myself first again. It was necessary, especially in grief.

After almost two full years of life in solitude and introspection, I felt ready to attract a partner into my life again. Because I was still relatively inexperienced in spiritual mind treatments, I turned to the assistant minister at my church, Rev. Karen Wolfson, for help. I figured that asking for relationship advice from another woman would be less intimidating. Her beautiful, strong spirit put me right at ease. To this day, she continues to play a significant role in my life as an older sister in our church family and close friend. Per my request, she performed a powerful mind treatment for me. I met John a few months later.

He ended up being one of the earliest demonstrations that came from my use of treatment work, which can also be thought of as affirmative prayer. It was a small investment of my energy that yielded rich results. I came from a sincere, genuine, concentrated place of heart and a pure desire to demonstrate a relationship like none I had ever experienced. The Infinite, with its unlimited field of possibility, exceeded all of my expectations. In my admittedly *limited* experience with such things, I had no idea what was reasonable to expect. I like to joke that the Universe brought him all the way from Connecticut to Georgia, just for me. It was serendipitous to say the least, and it opened my eyes up to the endless potentiality of what this Spirit can do.

Perhaps better said, what it could instruct *my* spirit to do. When I acknowledged the unlikeliness that my ideal guy would show up in my workplace (which was full of married men), or at my church (which had a large population of gay men), it was clear that I would have to put myself back in circulation. My goal was to find a hobby that would expose me to greater possibilities of meeting someone. Tennis came to mind. One, because it's a sport that I'd always wanted to learn, and two, because if nothing else it would provide some exercise. Sometimes you can feed two birds from the same hand.

After a handful of lessons, I was invited to a Round Robin one Sunday afternoon. Low and behold, so was John. He was a nice guy, attractive in every way I'd prayed for, and we found ourselves talking long after everyone else left. He and I swapped stories of the past; the challenging parts, the cherished parts, and everything in between. I felt compelled to bring up Science of Mind, but hesitated. I decided to ask him to go to church with me instead. Even though to this day he says he only went to be with me, he was intrigued and quickly got involved. The truth is the teaching filled a hole in his life as well. It wasn't long before he was immersed in learning all he could. The rest is history.

I flew to Oklahoma on business shortly after our marriage. My driver was an older, gentlemanly cowboy-type. There were many miles for us to go together before my destination, so naturally we struck up a conversation. He uttered a phrase that has remained in my heart ever since: "I picked my first wife, and God picked my second." I couldn't help but smile. Those words resonated with me to my core. I, too, had picked my first. And in that moment I realized that I had actually picked *every* other man in my life. But God picked John. That idea continued to swim in my head, until I came to the conclusion that *maybe I wasn't so good at picking*, and that surely this phenomenon wasn't exclusive to the realm of love. Attracting such a wonderful man like John into my life, by putting all of my faith into the Divine, gave me the courage to entrust IT with even more. It gave me the strength to release my own illusion of control. If there was to be anything heavenly in my life, I was going to have to let it come *to* me. In the thirty-four years that have passed since meeting John, so many other things have done the same. God's pick is *always* the right one.

INTENTION

Demonstrate a long lasting, loving relationship, unlike any I have ever experienced.

MIND TREATMENT

I now attract the right man who is in complete accord with me. This is a spiritual union because it is divine love functioning through the personality of someone with whom I blend perfectly. I know I can give this man love, light, peace, and joy. I feel and believe I can make this man's life full, complete, and wonderful. I now decree that he possess the following qualities and attributes:

He is spiritual, loyal, faithful, and true. He is harmonious, peaceful, happy, strong, powerful, loving, kind and ready for me. We are irresistibly attracted to each other.

Only that which belongs to love, truth and beauty can enter my experience. I accept my ideal companion now.

These are the words I repeated, over and over again. It is an adaptation of a treatment done by metaphysical teacher, writer, and speaker, Joseph Murphy, from *The Power of Your Subconscious Mind*. I personalized it to fit my exact needs and desires.

While we have undoubtedly grown over the course of our thirty-four years together, John continues to be a loving, supportive partner through and through. With similar religious backgrounds and unified spiritual beliefs, we have a strong spiritual foundation for our partnership to stand on. With us both being ministers, we have a shared career. Those words I said so long ago continue to blossom into new and exciting fruits in our relationship today. Just when I think it can't possibly get any better, it does. I am so thankful to have him by my side.

DEMONSTRATION

A life-long partner, and his whole, beautiful family.

Chapter Eight: A Calling

"At the height of your unique genius rests some masterpiece of splendor, laid out for you to do from the beginning, before ever the world was formed."

— Emma Curtis Hopkins

"...it's up to us to make ourselves available to the energy and intelligence that has patiently cultivated, over tens and thousands of years, our human capacity so it can take the next step through and as us."

— Andrew Cohen, *Evolutionary Enlightenment*

My spiritual journey eventually guided me to pursue studies in practitioner and ministerial programs. Up until then, I wasn't sure what I wanted to do with my life. Now, there seemed to be an invisible path leading me somewhere, gradually revealing itself just a few steps at a time. I couldn't help but follow it. This teaching breathed life into me in a way that nothing else I'd encountered ever had.

For many years, Centers for Spiritual Living held their annual conference at the beautiful Asilomar grounds in Pacific Grove, California. People came from all over the world to attend. I had heard about it since the beginning of my studies, and now, it was my turn to go.

My experience was heavenly. On the first glorious day, John and I flew into San Francisco where we were offered a Chrysler LeBaron convertible to rent at no extra charge. We stocked up on Ghirardelli's chocolate, and we followed a whale down the coast that continued to breach just for us. Being from the Midwest, I had never seen a whale in-person before, much less one *breaching*!

The retreat center, nestled right along the Pacific coastline with spectacular views of the Monterey Peninsula, was more than magical. Little did I know, the people I met that week would become lifelong friends. The conference was an incredible chance to exchange ideas with other people in the field, and in doing so, we were inspired to the greater possibilities of our own works back home.

My first trip to Asilomar was also particularly important because I would be taking my oral exams to become a licensed minister. The big day arrived, and I decided to explore the nature around the retreat in the hours before I was scheduled to meet my panel. I was drawn to the ocean. Natural water has such a calming, yet energizing, effect on me (two qualities I wanted to embody for this meeting), so this should've come as no surprise. I found a stunningly large rock to sit on, close to the water's edge. The coastline was dramatic, in a beautiful way—its swelling tides crashing forcibly against the shore before making their solemn retreat. It was the ideal place to be alone and have a talk with myself.

If my work had taught me anything at that point, it was the importance of spiritual preparation. I wanted to make sure I was clear. I had been preparing for this all my life, whether I knew it or not. All of the trials and tribulations, the highs and the lows, had been leading me to this next step. I let myself tune into the feeling of the rocks below me, standing calm and strong against the never-ending push and pull of the ocean. It was hard not to be inspired by the magnificent vision of the world before me. In that moment I knew. I was ready.

As I approached the meeting place for my interview, I was greeted by a minister who explained there had been a scheduling problem, and my interview would have to be moved to one of the ministers' rooms. To my surprise, I recognized all three of the members of my panel. We'd all been introduced the day before by the minister I could be replacing, Dr. Roy Graves.

As we engaged in small talk, I couldn't help but notice the view. The room we ended up in had a large sliding glass door that happened to be facing the exact rock I'd been sitting on earlier. The Universe had worked out the details, finding a way to assure me that all would be more than fine. I was not alone. I was in divine hands. The panel of seasoned ministers received me with warmth. I answered their questions with grace and ease. And through it all, I retained a crystal clear view of the rock that had granted me such a deep sense of support and stability, from beginning to end.

I could never have made any of that happen on my own, no matter how hard I tried. There were more moving pieces, parts, and players than I could control. The entire sequence reminded me once again that there was a bigger force at play, looking out for me. I couldn't have dreamed of it unfolding in a more perfect and enjoyable way.

This is how the Universal Spirit works. It takes in our heart's desire, our passions, our beliefs, and it manifests a corresponding landscape for us to live in. I relished in every delectable minute of my experience because I kept mindful of that presence. Life always reflects back to us what we know to be true without a shadow of a doubt. It always gives us what we truly need in order to evolve and expand towards our potential. That is the way! Our primary job is to prepare ourselves, take the time necessary to find alignment with the version of ourselves we want to be, and then trust in Spirit's ability to make it happen.

Of course, I passed with flying colors, and I am blessed to be writing about this—over 30 years later—in celebration of how far I have come. I love what I am doing, and I am grateful that I have been able to help so many people along the way.

After moving to Orlando, I took over a center there and John and I ran it together for the next twenty-five years. I feel compelled to call it an adventure. It certainly featured all of the themes that typically go along with one. We experienced some unquestionably difficult times and some incredible, unexpected highs that go beyond anything that I previously thought was possible in this world. All in all, it has been the most exciting journey I have ever been on.

INTENTION

To answer a call and become a minister

MIND TREATMENT

Knowing there was a perfect place and way for me to fulfill my purpose.

MEDITATION

Walking meditation & sitting on the beach.

IMAGINATION

Knowing I was a teacher from early on. Seeing myself help others return to wholeness. Contemplating the role.

DEMONSTRATION

Became a licensed (an eventually an ordained) minister for the Center for Spiritual Living in Orlando, Florida. John joined me in the ministry soon after, and together, we co-directed the center for a total of twenty-five years.

Chapter Nine: Joseph

"Undoubtedly, we are surrounded by, and immersed in, a perfect Life: a complete, normal, happy, sane, harmonious and peaceful existence. But only as much of this Life as we embody will really become ours to use."

— Ernest Holmes, *Science of Mind*

"When we are no longer able to change a situation, we are challenged to change ourselves."

— Viktor Frankl

There will be one or more times in this life when you absolutely cannot deny the Truth. One of my most indisputable *ah ha* moments came to me while I was trying to have a baby in my early 40s. The urge to conceive was consistent and powerful. The opportunity to become a mother again meant so much to me. Even though I had already been blessed with the births of two wonderful children, I missed out on a lot of their younger years due to us being physically separated during so much of that precious time. There was something incomplete about the way things went, something not quite finished for me.

Beyond the wisdom that often comes with age, I was also more aware of the challenges now than when I had first become a mom in my early twenties. I had more fears and doubts than I did then. Age was not the problem—women around the world were proving that. Italian singer Gianna Nannini was fifty-six when she gave birth to her first child in 2010. Carmela Bousada of Spain became one of the oldest mothers in 2006 when she had a baby in her mid-sixties. While the chances of conception drop considerably as women age, those percentages increase with fertility treatments and the assistance of medical intervention. In today's world, it's easy to lose sight of our connection with nature. Therefore, it's easier to lose confidence in our own natural abilities. Instead, we give away our power to every little thing that could possibly go wrong. Even though I knew better intellectually, emotionally I was no different than anyone else.

I lacked confidence in my body's capability. For me, the primary external triggers were discussions about the toxicity of microwaves and harmful chemicals in lipstick, diet sodas, pesticides and more. But internally, I was more susceptible to those talking points because of the deep personal guilt and shame about motherhood that I was still carrying close to my heart. Even though the memories of labor pains and postpartum symptoms were all but forgotten entirely, the relentless, haunting remorse I felt for being absent from my kids' early lives was still very much there. There were layers to unfold.

Being with a man who had no children of his own and was open to the idea of having one helped push me to begin peeling back those layers. It wasn't just about me, it was about us as a family; our shared journey together. He helped center me throughout the process of coming to terms with the reality that I potentially could be, and already was, in fact, a good mom. It was reassuring to have someone by side who, like me, felt somewhat apprehensive about the idea of raising a small child. I had somebody who I cherished and respected in my corner, reminding me that I was not alone or abnormal in my self-questioning. Neither of us had any idea what kind of adventure we were embarking upon when we said a decisive *yes* to the idea.

After my third miscarriage, our doctor called me into her office and asked, "What's up? Do you really want to have this baby?"

I knew what she was getting at. I said, "Yes, I really do want this baby, and I am working on something, personally, about it." I was not about to get into everything with her, as well-intentioned as she was. I knew I was getting close. I could feel it. Through the anguish of each and every miscarriage, I felt closer to where I needed to be. Each time I found myself having to go deeper, still, into my greatest fear.

So much of this time, I insisted on working this out myself. Staunch independence and self-reliance can get you in trouble. My teacher, Dr. Kennedy Shultz, after hearing of my troubles said, "I can't help you if I don't know what's going on". It was time to ask for help.

In response to my appeal, he wrote,

> *As far as the miscarriage is concerned, I wouldn't psychologize yourself to death over it. It leads into duality, and that is what we are so diligent about teaching people to move away from. There is no one keeping score on your life and deciding whether or not you deserve to have another child. If this were the way the law worked, child bearing on this planet would have come to a halt a long time ago. I think your treatment needs to be designed to create a mental equivalent of yourself and John as loving people eager to make a commitment to let a child come into this world and live beautifully by means of your love, and your wisdom. You both have done much to develop that love and wisdom, and you want to use it now creatively in all things. IT IS THAT SIMPLE!!! Remember, the Law doesn't know 'deserve'. It only knows 'desire' backed up by 'belief' in the rightness of the desire.*

Months later, he emailed me a mind treatment:

> *I realize that the unfailing Creator of all that can be, moving creatively through my open mind and heart, has made me an ideal mother to my children, and a perfect prospect for bringing new life into the world as a new and beautiful child.*

As the womb of my consciousness is alight with pure vitality and clear understanding, the womb of my body is a warm and nurturing and beautifully functioning place. It is a fitting place for a new life to begin and a safe place for a new life to take form.

The radiance of this right recognition of me as an ideal mother shines through all negative experience. It is the real and the only creative power at work in my life.

I accept it. I recognize it. And I let it be so. And so it is!

Each time I read it, my confidence grew. Several months later, I got pregnant again. The hard part wasn't over, of course, but something about this one felt different. Whenever I started to fret or worry about potential complications, I reminded myself that all I needed was faith the size of a mustard seed. Surely, I had that much.

John and I started playing with names. We decided that if it was a girl, we would call her Emmalee. John always knew that if he had a son, his name would be Joseph. It didn't matter that we already had two Joes on my side of the family. I let it go as I had my pick of names with my first two. I always liked the name Joseph.

One morning after our Sunday Celebration, I walked into the Youth room to teach a class and came across a lone colored picture on the table, signed with the name Emmalee. As far as I knew, there were not any new children in the class that day. I put the picture in my briefcase and forgot about it. Over the next couple days, I did some inquiry, and no one seemed to know anything about an Emmalee.

Early that week, I was going through my briefcase and ran across the big blue egg, signed *Emmalee*. I couldn't help but think about it throughout the rest of the day. It was so strange. It conjured up something unfamiliar within me, something that felt significant, but that I didn't fully understand. It was almost like a personal message to me from God, or Emmalee herself. Over the course of that day she became real to me. She had my attention.

Later that same day, I was preparing to teach a class and felt drawn to a section in the Science of Mind textbook that discusses the nature of God and what IT does. This is the passage that jumped out to me:

Here and now, we are surrounded by, and immersed in, an Infinite Good. How much of this Infinite Good is ours? ALL OF IT! And how much of IT may we have to use? AS MUCH OF IT AS WE CAN EMBODY.

In a flash, I put two and two together. Connecting the dots, making it all clear. I had not embodied, emotionally, a baby. In the undeniable face of this Truth, I cried. I had not let myself get into full synchrony with the idea of a new child in my life. I was holding myself emotionally back from it. It was *my* foot pushing down on the brake, not God's. I wasn't allowing myself to fully believe in the reality I desired, just in case it didn't happen. I still had an unaddressed resistance to the idea, for fear that I, or my child, would get hurt again.

I had to stand clear and firm in my belief of the truth of my heart's desire. I knew how much it meant to me, and I longed to fulfill it. We all do. We all know what it feels like to be denied an opportunity. It's a scary possibility, but it is an unproductive one to entertain. I had been working on myself, mentally and spiritually, but I hadn't taken it far enough. The guarded part of my heart had to open up. I had to become vulnerable before I could demonstrate a reality that still felt somewhat out of reach.

I will never forget that realization. An *ah ha* of that magnitude is one of those things you can't understand until you experience it for yourself. I liken it to my first couple years of having sex, when I wasn't having orgasms. I didn't know I was supposed to be having them, or what they even were. I thought I was having the full experience, until I finally did, and then I understood. In the case of my efforts to conceive, I *thought* I was as open to the idea as I could be. But now, I understood how much I'd been holding back. On every level, I felt my heart stretch and expand in a way it hadn't before. I didn't have to know how or why, all I knew for sure was that it had happened.

What are the chances that two random events would grab my attention on the same day—invoking pure love and challenging my deepest fears—and culminate in a cathartic epiphany related to my current situation? Next to none. But that is what the Universe does. It bucks probability when it comes to your heart's desires. IT will find a way to get you there, even if you're standing in your own way. IT will usher you to a place beyond the limits of where you think you can go.

This third pregnancy was something that wanted and needed to happen as a part of my spiritual journey. I thought I wanted a baby. That was a form. The *soul's desire* behind that form was to be healed and returned to wholeness, even if I couldn't consciously recognize it at the time.

I concluded that this time would be my last and final try. My body had been through so much already. If it wasn't going to happen with a baby, it would happen another way, because this was something that wanted to be released.

Interestingly, the crayoned image was of a blue egg. Emmalee obviously did not take form in our lives. Joseph did. Maybe Joseph is Emmalee, turned boy. Maybe John needed to experience a son. Only God knows. To us, it really didn't matter. We were beyond elated at the prospect of our deepest desire finally growing into a full-formed reality.

The Thing ITself will always give us more than we expect. IT exists to inspire. My heart was opened even wider. I was able to be even more present with my older children through the birth of another. An even greater love emerged between us, which acted as a bridge between the gap of time we'd lost, and made way for a new, more healed kind of relationship that reached beyond what any of us had previously imagined was possible.

INTENTION

To bring new life into the world through us.

AFFIRMATIONS

I fully trust and embody my true heart's desires knowing they are already mine.

I have faith the size of a mustard seed.

TREATMENT

I realize that the unfailing Creator of all that can be, moving creatively through my open mind and heart, has made me an ideal mother to my children and a perfect prospect for bringing new life into the world as a new and beautiful child. As the womb of my consciousness is alight with pure vitality and clear understanding, the womb of my body is a warm and nurturing and beautifully functioning place. It is a fitting place for a new life to begin and a safe place for a new life to take form. The radiance of this right recognition of me as an ideal mother shines through all negative experience. It is the real and the only creative power at work in my life. I accept it. I recognize it. And I let it be so. And so it is!

DEMONSTRATION

Joseph Elliot DePalma was born on January 23, 1998. A beautiful baby boy who continues to be a blessing to our family.

Chapter Ten: A Retreat to the Canadian Rockies

"The good that is for you loves you as much as you love it. The good that is for you seeks you and will come flying to you if you see that what you love is love itself."

— Emma Curtis Hopkins

"As a single footstep will not make a path on the earth, so a single thought will not make a pathway in the mind. To make a deep physical path, we walk again and again. To make a deep mental path, we must think over and over the kind of thoughts we wish to dominate our lives."

— Henry David Thoreau

Fast-forward to 2007. Joseph was turning nine, and John and I had been running the Center for thirteen years. We were both fortunate to have found work we loved. However, our household income was entirely reliant on our community's donations and, as one can imagine, that amount was constantly in flux. Just about everything John and I had taken home over the last decade-and-a-third had been relative to the prosperity of our members.

I made the decision to introduce a new class on *The Four Spiritual Laws of Abundance* by Edwene Gaines, with the hope that greater abundance in our members' lives, as well as our own, could potentially translate into more for us all. During my time with the class, I got word of an upcoming trip being organized by a spiritual mentor and friend, Mary Morrissey, to the Canadian Rockies. I was enrolled in her advanced self-mastery class, and she had just finished hosting a workshop on self-empowerment at our Center, and I really wanted to go on this trip. It was postured to be an intimate spiritual retreat set against the breathtaking natural landscapes of the province of Alberta. It sounded incredible, but I didn't see how it would be possible for me to attend. The trip itself, with lodging at the historical Chateau Isabella, the activities, and my airfare would cost approximately two thousand dollars. And even if money hadn't been a concern, my mother's condition was getting worse.

Three years earlier, she'd been diagnosed with myelofibrosis, a rare cancer of the blood. Her need for transfusions had increased dramatically over the last few months. They were the closest thing to a remedy at the time. She'd have good days, then bad days, and then good days following another transfer. Now there are more effective treatments, but in 2007, the survival rate was offensively low. From the point of diagnosis, patients would be given a life expectancy of one to fifteen years. We all knew that it was just a matter of time. I'd call her to do mind treatments over the phone as often as she'd allow me to, which averaged about once a week. I decided to let the trip idea simmer until I had more clarity.

After another session of our new class on *The Four Spiritual Laws of Abundance* concluded one Sunday, a member who'd been attending our church for several years—and was known to take the practice of tithing very seriously—tapped me on the shoulder. I turned to face her, expecting a question or commentary on the day's material. You can imagine my surprise when she handed me a sealed envelope with a gratified smile on her face. She leaned in and whispered, "I want you to have this."

When I got home, I opened it, and my jaw hit the floor. It was a check for two thousand dollars. She later explained to me that she'd inherited an unexpected sum of money from a relative. She wanted to share it with me, in gratitude for all she was learning in the new class. I was speechless.

The retreat was set to take place in less than two months, but even with the means to go, I still had to contend with the notion of leaving the country for ten days with my mother in a worsening condition. Having just spent two weeks with her in Columbia, South Carolina, immersed not only in the logistics of the inevitable, but the first inklings of the weighty emotions that were sure to follow, I really needed a break. The three years since her diagnosis had been a nonstop rollercoaster for everyone in my family, especially her.

Throughout every day, for many days, I debated whether to go or not. I meditated and prayed about it incessantly, and eventually, the fears I had surrounding the risks began to subside. I felt confident in saying yes to the serendipitous opportunity that was presenting itself. I trusted in the feeling that this trip would function as a much needed preparation for what was yet to come. I knew that I would need to be as strong as I could be when that day finally came. I trusted that her spirit would wait.

After the decision was made, all of the other details came together almost effortlessly. I flew into Calgary that August, met up with the rest of the group, and we all had a chance to introduce ourselves before hopping on a bus to the little town of Beazer, our homebase for the next week-and-a-half. The Chateau was more than able to accommodate all fifteen of us, and we got to spend a considerable amount of time getting to know the owner. She was a woman about my mother's age who had been given the gift of the Chateau by her husband, Harry. Harry picked us up from the airport and drove us all around the countryside for our excursions in a big bus owned by the estate. Marion, her daughter, and the staff made sure we came back to scrumptious home-cooked meals. One night Marion shared her own story of hardship, spiritual transformation, and healing. Spirit was close to her; we could all feel it. She reminded me so much of my mother.

Although the name *Chateau Isabella* implied an indulgent luxury, the space was incredibly homey, well-cared for, and relaxed. It was the only man-made structure in the area, as far as our eyes could see, and the property itself was outlined by the stunningly regal Rocky Mountains. At night, the skies were so dark and unobstructed that you could witness tens of thousands of sparkling stars, all at once. No televisions, no radios, just natural connection. It's one of those places you wished you never had to leave.

One of our first day trips led us back over the U.S. border into Glacier National Park. Spiritually, the number thirteen signifies a time of completion and renewal, where beginning meets the end, and standing alone, staring at the magnificent beauty of the mountains, I realized that I'd stood in this park thirteen years ago. I had arrived a day early for my first minister's conference so I could venture out and take in some of this outstanding beauty without a time constraint. As I stood face to face with the landscape, I lost myself in awestruck wonderment. I could have spent the rest of my time there just staring at their magnificence. And here it was again.

My mind could hardly help comparing the two versions of myself that had showed up here. Standing at the foothills, I appreciated how far I'd truly come. The person I was today existed on the other side of some of the roughest parts of my life's journey thus far, including letting go of my Dad, and having another baby in the midst of an active ministry. I was now a well-seasoned traveler. I was now capable of making good decisions, with the help of the Universe. I let out a sigh of relief. I had accomplished so much. I had grown tremendously. How perfectly orchestrated and divinely set up was this celebration of me. I stood in awe and wonder at the magnificence of Life and how IT works. *Thank you, Universe, for this wonderful life I have been given and who I am because of all of my life experiences!*

It turns out that going on this trip was the best decision I could have made. This retreat to the Canadian Rockies, staying at the unforgettable Chateau Isabella, and then driving farther north up to see the magnificent Banff Mountains, was spectacular. This time away deeply fed my soul, giving me a chance to rest and recharge. I knew the time was drawing close to saying good-bye to my Mom, the one person who had always been there for me. This escape fortified me through her transition, and after. Now, I was ready. As ready as anyone can hope to be in these situations.

Her soul had waited for me, as I knew it would. She passed about two months after I returned, that November.

INTENTION

Increase my prosperity consciousness, individually and collectively for our center by teaching the "Four Spiritual Laws of Abundance", and give my mother my best love and attention during her transition.

IMAGINATION

I felt a definite call to go to the Canadian Rockies with one of my favorite teachers. I studied the pictures and imagined what that might be like to go.

DEMONSTRATION

Time away to retreat in the Canadian Rockies, with my main expenses covered.

Chapter Eleven: Africa Calls

"Your search is after something great enough to lose your littleness in, something within you worthy of immortality and eternal expansion."

— Ernest Holmes, *This Thing Called You*

"We must be willing to let go of the life we have planned, so that we can have the life that is waiting for us."

— Joseph Campbell

"...everything you want, wants you!"

— Genevieve Behrend

It all started at an Asilomar conference in Monterey, California—John and I had invited all three of the children to come along with us for the week-long festivities. Joseph was enrolled in a youth-focused program there, and Nic and Liz enjoyed the camp-like setting, three square meals a day with delicious comfort foods, the beach, and the freeform dance class they were taking together. We all decided to go for a walk around the grounds one day towards the end of the trip, and our eyes were drawn to a booth that had been set up outside of the conference bookstore. The table was full of handwoven baskets and cloths with bright and intricate designs, organic coffee beans, jewelry pieces made out of string and colored beads, and carved soapstone figurines. We were greeted by the friendly couple running the booth, who introduced themselves to us as Kathy Hamilton and Floyd Hammer. You never know when you are about to cross paths with the catalyst of your destiny. It would take years before I could appreciate the impact this chance encounter would have on my life's trajectory.

It was clear that Kathy and Floyd were passionate about their work in Tanzania—their enthusiasm was contagious. On their most recent trip, the organization they had founded, The Outreach Program, had built its first school and resource center in a Tanzanian village so that the local children could study and rely on at least one nutrient-dense meal every day. Other past trips involved projects to create sustainable and safe water networks that could easily be accessed by villages in need, and to construct and reconstruct school buildings—as well as medical missions where they would take volunteer doctors, nurses, and teachers with them.

Their upcoming trip was a pediatric medical mission that was set to depart in August – just a few months away. I was assured that even though I wasn't a medical professional, there would be plenty to do in support of the medical staff, in addition to interacting with children and their families while they were waiting to be seen. I first fell in love with Africa on the spot, just hearing about all they did. When Africa gets into your heart, it makes a stronghold. I wanted in. I vowed right then and there that I would go with them on one of their trips as soon as I could, even if it wasn't the one in August. Liz was right there with me. The desire was there, but we both knew the timing wasn't quite right. We needed time to grow into the idea. She would go years after me, after finishing nursing school.

I was concerned about the large sum of money required to make such a trip. Floyd assured me that coming up with the money was the easy part. I didn't understand at first, but he was right. The money came at the perfect time, about two years after I'd planted the seed. It was the mental and physical preparations that kept me busy—the many different vaccinations required and collecting and packing all the things I might need while I was there.

Thank God an angel of a nurse helped me through all the shots. I am not big on shots—I used to faint in grade school waiting in the lines to get them— but I was determined nothing was going to stop me from going!

As I prepared, more questions came up…*What if I get sick? What if I get injured?* My imagination ran away with me. I had never been that far away from home. There were things in my mind I needed to get straight before going. The trip was going to be arduous enough, and I didn't have to make it worse.

I was on a timeline. As my trip to Africa got closer and I collected what I needed for my trip, I was still concerned that I wouldn't have everything I needed. Part of the confusion was that I received a very long list of medical supplies that I might need. I was one of the few people going who was not part of the medical profession. It's quite possible that I didn't need to bring all that I did. I never asked. I did not know how rough it was there, so I thought it wouldn't hurt to have extra medical supplies with me. If nothing else, I would leave them there for those in need.

Heavy in my head, I walked through my favorite local wildlife reserve. Frank, a ranger friend pulled up in his utility truck alongside me and asked me how I was. I shared my angst with him. He reassured me that I would have everything I needed. If I didn't, there would be a way to get it. Those words immediately settled my troubled mind. He was God speaking to me that day. Sure enough, something *did* pop up that I needed when I was there. More about that later.

It was time. My wonderful husband, John, agreed to take charge of our 11-year-old son, our home, and all the responsibilities of running a spiritual center, for which I will always be grateful! Having everything in place, I was ready for an adventure. I was ready for a *vision quest* as Sam, my treatment partner, called it—ready to see more of myself and more of the bigger picture to which I belong, with more direction, clarity, and consciousness. What's more, I was ready to 'go it' alone.

My daughter wanted so badly to go along with me, but she was preparing for nursing school, and knew that it was still not yet her time. I told her that I would check things out first, and that her time would come.

I looked forward to experiencing myself in a deeper, more expansive way. I was excited to get to know my sisters and brothers across the ocean, and to learn about how they lived. I had had enough of the materialism of our culture. I wanted to see how people with little or nothing could live and find happiness. What was their secret? I needed to know. I also wanted to get in touch with the genuineness and purity of their spirit. And with my own.

IDEAL DAY - JANUARY 10TH, 2009

I am prepared, as prepared as I need to be with what is here, what I am taking and with where I am going. This is a Life Quest or Vision Quest. This is part two. The first being my retreat to the Canadian Rockies. I am ready to have doors open in my heart and head that need to be there that were not there before. I am ready to come back significantly changed, and in the meantime, to give as much as I can possibly give to your people—to YOU, through your people.

IDEAL DAY - JANUARY 13TH, 2009

Universe, I am ready to experience my Vision Quest, this personal journey into you! I am thrilled to have everything I need to take this journey. I am determined to stay present and focused and have an amazing experience. I experience the fullest possible experience of YOU I can have. I fully trust I have the clarity, strength, love, courage, power, energy, health, and wealth to be fully present and give of myself completely. I am grateful for the gift in advance. I fully trust and know that you are in charge and perfectly expanding and growing your people and our services more and more.

JOURNAL EXCERPT - JANUARY 16TH, 2009

I am here in Africa. It doesn't seem real. It didn't seem real crossing the Atlantic Ocean at night and spending time in the Amsterdam airport, waiting for our final flight over Germany, Greece, Cairo, into Mount Kilimanjaro, Tanzania. We were in a huge plane that seemed to land in the middle of nowhere, in the dark. It was evening there. The temperature was about 76 degrees. I remember going through my suitcase in the parking lot trying to figure out what I was going to need. They wanted us to just take what we needed for the next 24 hours. The big luggage was going ahead of us to our destination.

That night, we stayed at the Kilimanjaro International Airport Lodge; a beautiful place with hut-style rooms, mosquito netting around the beds, beautiful rock pathways, gardens of cacti, trees, and purple bougainvillea (my favorite flower). There were even some freshly picked and laid out for decoration on our beds.

President Obama's Inauguration was going on while we were there. At one point before my departure, I asked myself…why was I going to Africa, of all places, exactly at the time of the inauguration? I wanted to be a part of that, too. It was a high point in our nation's history to be electing an African-American man as its leader, a hard-fought freedom. And here I was, traveling from America to Africa. It seemed to be an auspicious moment. I knew there had to be a reason, and I was anxious to see what the Universe had in mind.

On the day of the Inauguration, a group of us were shopping in the marketplace in Singida. It was late afternoon and we saw people watching the pre-inauguration on old TVs set up on the dirt floors of their little shacks. There were posters of Obama everywhere. Later, we got to enjoy the speech that night on CNN in the lobby of the Catholic Social Center where we stayed. Yes, on the other side of the world, in a third-world country, we, as a country, were being watched!

What I loved about The Outreach Program was that we were there to *be* together and serve in whatever way we could. We were not there to convert anyone. That is not what this organization does. If we believe that everyone is our equal, and the same Power and Intelligence that runs through our veins is running through theirs, there is no need for conversion. We support others in believing in themselves and we trust that God is at work everywhere. No one is left behind. When we are sure of ourselves, there is nothing we *need* to do. We do whatever we do out of the great love and joy within us.

Our first Sunday there, Floyd, my friend and co-director of The Outreach Program, took me over to the Lutheran Church in Singida for the late service. One of our team, who I believe was Lutheran, was speaking. The head Pastor was out of town on business. Floyd introduced me to the Youth Minister who was in charge that day, as a fellow minister. Before I knew it, I was clothed in a white robe and walking up the aisle from the back of the church, in a procession, with my tennis shoes on. I had no idea that I was going to be so involved! Three of us, two other clergy and myself, squeezed onto the very small kneeler before the altar. I got as skinny as I possibly could. Then, I got to experience a whole different kind of service, with dancing, singing, a talk in Swahili, and the biggest baskets I ever saw for an offering, big enough to include the first fruits of the harvest. It truly was an event.

At the end of the service, the youth minister invited me to speak the following Sunday, the day we were set to leave. Of course I said yes! During the week, our team was invited to a social at the church where I was pushed onto the floor by an American to be one of the first dancers, (thank you American, and thank you to me for saying sometime prior that I wanted to learn how to dance again). By the time it was over, everyone was dancing and having fun. Then, we were invited to go talk in another room where they had prepared refreshments for us: a small, glass bottle of original coke and some fried hors d'oeuvres.

I was seated at a table for the main guests, next to the Pastor, whom I was meeting for the first time. He gave me a very serious look over. Our first meeting was awkward. First, I was a 'female minister' in a traditional church. Second, I was not of a 'traditionally recognized' denomination. Third, it was his youth minister who invited me to speak that Sunday. He had been given no choice in the matter.

I decided to give him a way out: "I know I was invited by your youth minister. You didn't have a choice." While I was excited, (and petrified at the same time), about such a wonderful opportunity, "I do not *have* to do it." I was on a peace mission with no agenda. He said nothing.

The formal gathering began. We introduced ourselves to the room and said what we were grateful for: *I was grateful for my wonderful husband at home, who was taking care of our child, our home, and our community. I would not be here today with all these wonderful people if it wasn't for him.*

Well, whatever I said changed things for him and after everyone was finished, he turned to me and said, "You can speak for my people next Sunday."

I was honored; then, it hit me, what was I going to say in a conservative church, to people of a different culture and background, that would be meaningful to them and not offend anyone in the process? Not to mention, I don't speak Swahili!

Their theme for the year was "God is Good all the time. All the time, God is Good".

That was my intention…something meaningful to them, a universal message that went beyond the barriers of religion, culture, and even language. I intended to love and serve. As Rumi puts it so eloquently, *"Out beyond ideas of wrong doing and right doing, there is a field. I will meet you there."* That is what we did—met them together in that magnificent field beyond.

MIND TREATMENT - JANUARY 24TH, 2009

(the day before my talk at the church in Singida)

Universe, I am ready to deliver a life changing message from you to the people of the world. I am an open, receptive channel through which you speak. I am receptive, clear-minded, focused, and ready to receive and deliver the greatest message possible in order to infuse great love, here, as my gift to my brothers and sisters of the world. I am ready to step into my next larger playing field.

Thank you, thank you, thank you for the great gift I have been given – the gift of who I am. Thank you for the great gift I have come to bring. Thank you for the great gift I give. Thank you for helping the gift be received. Thank you for helping me to come from a genuine place of heart. Thank you for the perfect unfoldment of this day, for tomorrow, for this trip, for John and for my ministry at large. Thank you for smooth days while I am away from home, and especially on Sundays.

Today, I take the next steps, I listen. I meditate. I write. I read. I pack. I organize. I leave what I am leaving here. I enjoy it. I love myself. I am open to receiving. Thank you for taking care of John, Joseph, Nic and Liz, my family. I wholeheartedly embrace all this and more, now and forevermore. Thank you God! And so it is! I am grateful for the warm hospitality, affection, and love of these people.

The morning of my talk, I woke up with the direction I would take. Thank you, God!

IDEAL DAY - JANUARY 25TH, 2009

I step confidently into this day with complete rest and trust in myself and God knowing I am guided and supported every step of the way. The words I speak, today, are healing words. They are intimate and they are good. It is my intention to speak from love and give a message of love, with love to myself and others.

Then, I got a call. The young man who was to be my interpreter had to work. There was nothing I could do. This was going to be interesting. I just had to laugh, release, and let go. This was definitely out of my hands.

Halfway through the service, a man approached me on the altar during some singing and dancing and said he would be my interpreter. Thank you, God, once again!

It seemed a little bit bold to bring up politics in church, in a foreign land but I have learned to trust what comes to me and so I did...I shared with them my excitement of having Barack Obama as our new president. I said I believed that he was not only talking to the American people, he was talking to the people of the world. His message was for us all to BE MORE and live from a higher place...to work together...to take more responsibility...to have courage...to say the hard-to-say things and to take the necessary steps.

I told them that during my visit I could see their challenges and difficulties, and that even though Americans have more physical comforts and money, they, too, had different kinds of challenges and difficulties. Many of OUR PEOPLE have lost their way in physical possessions and gotten distracted by material things, lost touch with their roots, and forgotten who they are.

We all have work to do. We have much to learn from each other and to share.

It is going to take the Christ Consciousness or Spirit in us—that strength, power, wisdom, and love—to move us out of our problems and into solutions.
With God's help, WE CAN DO IT! YES WE CAN!

We were ONE.

We are FAMILY.

We are all living the ONE LIFE OF GOD.

Change for the better is already happening.

God's infinite Intelligence is shaking things up, helping us to let go of old, limiting beliefs, and helping us to grow and bring out our best.

There is great wealth that lies here, in our hearts...deep resources within.

We can no longer sit on the sidelines waiting for someday or for someone else to do something for us.

We have been given great gifts and we must pray to have eyes to see them.

Seeing them will bring more to life. Gratitude will bring more.

God is always with you, ...inspiring, guiding, directing even when you can't see or believe, even when you don't understand God's way.

We must choose the right thinking, good thoughts. Thoughts are our continuous prayers to God.

In the 10 days we were here, our medical team of 34 doctors, nurses, and lay people took care of 950 children and adults. There were many more that were turned away. We did not have the resources to take care of everyone. Some people wait years for doctors or surgeons from other countries to help them with their physical problems, deformities, and medical issues. I wanted them to know that we were not Gods and that if GOD is good all the time, there had to be other solutions to their problems, regardless of our presence, right where they are.

Next, I talked specifically to the youth after working with some very wonderful young people who were our translators throughout our stay. I told the youth they had a very special gift to give. That they were important. They needed to stay open, study hard, and learn God's truth—Universal Truth.

"Remember you are a gift to the world. You have something special to share. Remember. Pray for guidance."

Later that morning, as we walked out to their courtyard, Pastor Makalla told me that he liked how gentle I was with his people and that I was invited to come back and speak again.

Later that day, we said goodbye to Singhida. As we traveled to one of the wildlife reserves, we saw pictures of Obama on the back of buses, and under it, was written, "In God We Trust".

In God WE Trust! *Asante Sana!* (*'Thank you very much'* in Swahili)

Another surprise from the Universe: I rode a camel. A good friend from my first days in Science of Mind sent me a Christmas card with him and his family riding camels in Egypt. Years ago I said to Sam, my treatment partner, "I want a life where I get to ride camels! Before leaving the county, I had the opportunity and went for it! Even though it took years to come to pass, the Universe remembered. As soon as I was in the vicinity, IT made it happen!

As we approached our first wildlife reserve, giraffe heads peeked out from the trees to greet us. This brought a huge smile to my face as years before Liz and Nic, my oldest children, gave us a beautiful wooden giraffe and her baby as a gift. That piece has been on our mantel ever since. I stare at it all the time! Again, the Universe remembered, and as soon as I was close enough, IT came out to play with me in the form of tall, gorgeous giraffes.

It turns out I needed a pair of shoes to wear for the Sunday I was speaking. One of our translators agreed to take me to the marketplace and help me find shoes. Not finding much, he thought of a new store to try, an actual building. I didn't find a pair of shoes there, but I did find a pair of dressier sandals that would work. Those sandals fit me better than the ones I find in the States! European sizing works better for my narrow feet! Who would have guessed I would find a better fit there, which was comfortable, as well!

What I experienced were beautiful, loving, generous people, adorable children, rich, lush, expansive lands, and a deep appreciation for us being there for them. I don't remember feeling this much at home, in our country. I was touched at a very deep level.

What I experienced was the trip of a lifetime. Even though I had no idea at the time, I had been preparing for it all my life. What I found there was exactly what I needed to find!

JOURNAL EXCERPT FROM JUST BEFORE THE TRIP

It's time to give more of myself to the world, larger gifts, using my opportunities to come together with others at times to really make the most of who I am. Universe, I invite you to use me, to put me before those who are ready to hear the Truth, ready to see a bigger picture, ready to be consoled, encouraged, and inspired. I am ready to speak in public more frequently. I am ready to be interviewed. I am ready for my gift book to be released to the world. I am ready to travel. I am ready to teach. I am ready to exemplify. I am more present and available, "on the spot" to be your perfect channel than ever. I AM. I am my own authority. I am ready to speak to people who really want to be talked with, see people who really want to be seen, and love people who really want to be loved. I am ready to dance!

JOURNAL EXCERPT FROM THE LAST DAYS OF THE TRIP

Thank you for this amazing journey. It is absolutely an incredible experience. It changed me long before I came. Just thinking about it brought up so much emotion in me. Thank you for another magnificent day. Every day it becomes clearer to me about my own purpose here and the direction of my life's work. I am so grateful for my perfect health and wholeness, strength, power, energy, clarity of mind, wisdom, love and compassion. I am grateful for perfect direction, powerful new friendships and partnerships. They are truly life-changing, which I appreciate all day long and for the rest of my life. Thank you, Spirit, for calling and for that spirit in me being alive and awake enough to answer, to see that this was for me.

I know Africa lives in my heart. I know I am changed forever. I know that whatever I need to know about my participation there, here, or wherever, I know. I follow your lead. You continue to use me in amazing ways and for that I am so grateful. Kwaheri, farewell. And sala'am ala'ikum, peace be upon you all!

INTENTION

To answer a call, to serve, to explore the world, to step into a larger picture of me.

DEMONSTRATION

A deepening of my soul, and a highly successful and heartwarming trip to Africa.

Chapter Twelve: Community Outreach

"Every difficulty carries with it the wherewithal for its overcoming!

When you make a failure, it is because you have not asked enough; keep on and a larger thing than you were seeing will certainly come to you. Remember this." — Wallace D. Wattles

"If this time-space reality has within it the ability to inspire a desire within you, it is absolute that this time-space reality has the ability to yield you a full and satisfying manifestation of that same desire. It is Law."

— Esther Hicks/Abraham, *Money and the Law of Attraction*

When I returned home from Tanzania, more than one person asked me, "How could you stand seeing children starving in the streets?" It was an understandable question to have, but the more I thought about it, the more it revealed to me about our complex human nature. There's a sort of paradox that we may find ourselves in when we are an observer to an undesirable, desperate, or seemingly hopeless situation that we are not experiencing firsthand. On the one hand, we feel a pull to help and heal whatever it is (whether a person, place, or thing) that we can recognize as being ill, injured, or otherwise out of order. On the other hand, we feel powerless. There is only so much we can do.

Instinctually, there is a part of us that tries to protect our own heart from the heart-wrenching. It is undoubtedly easier to care from a distance, or talk at endless lengths about the need for *somebody* to make a positive change, but without ever getting up close and personal, we miss the opportunity to experience our humanity. We miss the opportunity to connect with one another on a human level which is what we all desire at some level whether we know it or not.

For my first time at the feeding center in Tanzania, a wonderful nurse named Laurie tossed me a bottle of bubbles without saying a word. Without questioning why she had, I got to work on blowing bubbles. Within a few minutes, most (if not all) of the children were running and screaming in an unspoken formation through the bubbles. Laurie and I were the only two who got to experience this authentic moment of joy with them. A handful of our team members who hadn't were worried that we were making a scene. The thought didn't cross my mind. All I could feel at that moment was appreciation. For each one of those precious few minutes, I was experiencing a reality beyond starvation, homelessness, poverty, illness, death, and fear, and so were they. It was there that my heart cracked open. So in answer to the question, "How can I see any good in the bad?" Because of love, there is a place beyond conditions where we can meet and see each other for the strong, beautiful, unbridled spirits we are.

Kathy and Floyd had a similar experience in that sense. In 2003, they were first invited to Africa to help convert a hospital that specialized in leprosy into a hospital for AIDS patients. During that trip, Kathy had an opportunity to help out at another hospital where she saw, firsthand, child after child die of starvation. The feelings that experience held for her were a fire that inspired her and Floyd's change in career path. It was as soon as she saw her husband again that she approached him with an unconditional certainty.

"Floyd, we have to do something."

He wholeheartedly agreed.

Their first initiative was to build a school: a singular, but effective step in breaking the cycle of poverty. Not long after beginning the project, they were able to see with their own eyes that basic resources like nutrient-rich food and clean water were a bigger priority. Lives were at stake. The country did not have the financial freedom to build a thoughtful, efficient, sustainable infrastructure in every area of the land that would benefit from it, but Kathy and Floyd knew that for them to make a positive, sustainable change, it would have to be one that the Tanzanians could financially sustain on their own. Kathy and Floyd started searching for the true sources of value for the people who were experiencing a heart-wrenching and seemingly hopeless reality. Right off the bat, they saw the gorgeous baskets that the Tanzanian women would weave in their free time. The designs were unique, intricate, and beautiful. Later on, they were able to experience the rich, natural, Arabica mountain coffee that grows along the shaded, northern slopes of Mount Kilimanjaro and Mount Meru. They didn't have to make any major changes, just small ones. Throughout the decades of time and energy that they've devoted to growing The Outreach Program, they have been able to help thousands of Tanzanians emphasize the parts of themselves and their ecosystem that were already abundant, strong, and healthy.

Regarding our own Center for Spiritual Living, someone once said to me, "You have a great center and a wonderful group of people but you are not involved in the greater community."

At the time, I felt like my capacity to do for others was nearly maxed out. I was doing everything I could to keep up with what was already on my plate. And at the time, I wasn't feeling called to any specific community cause.

One minister outside of my church urged me to take part in the effort against the unfair treatment of workers in Central Florida. Although my heartstrings were being pulled because the cause needed attention, I knew in my heart that it wasn't the right step for *me* to take. Nevertheless, I decided to open up my mind to the idea of such a commitment. I waited, trusting, for that feeling. The moment I met Kathy and Floyd, it appeared. My affiliation with The Outreach Program was exactly like that. My experience with them has progressed so organically, so naturally, and so enjoyably, that it would be wholly impossible for my heart ever to second-guess or regret the time I've spent with them and The Outreach Program.

While there are many worthwhile causes in the world, we can only do so much. Getting into alignment with those that call us is key. Imagine what the world would look like if everyone did that. There is something for everyone.

After my first experience in Africa, coming home and realizing that *this* was the opportunity to heal that was in my heart, I called Kathy and Floyd with the hope that one of them had any ideas. I couldn't do exactly what they were doing. I couldn't keep traveling to Africa and back every couple of months. I had an abundant, strong, and healthy life in the States. I wanted to dedicate my time to making a positive change, but I needed to do it in a way that was authentic for me.

They told me that they were currently looking for a sizable community of people in the States to help with volunteer food packaging. The nutritious food packaged by the volunteers in day-long community events would later be shipped in containers to Tanzania. The first thought that came to my mind was the Center. *This* was a way for me to engage the community in action, in a way that was authentic and enriching to our understanding of the core principles we study.

There comes a point on our spiritual path where we long to experience ourselves on a deeper, authentic level. A great way to accomplish this is through the strengthening of our relationship with the world around us. If we are without a meaningful, deep connection to some aspect of our greater community, whether that community is big or small, we are denying ourselves one of the most powerful connections that a human being can experience. It's more powerful than passionately talking about or confidently presuming one's life philosophy. There is no need in it for debate. This feeling of connection is only possible in a combination of *loving passion* and *action* when we decide to *be* and *do* something about it.

> *There will come a time when you will not use words. No words can truly express your understanding of God: You are it – and what understanding of God you feel, is the substance that you show.*
>
> —Emma Curtis Hopkins

It is a tricky business opening hearts. We ran the risk of getting caught up in the adverse conditions ourselves. We see more of what we choose to focus on, so it was important for us to be clear about what we wanted to see happen for us next. Why take the chance of getting involved in the first place and risk the potential of finding ourselves in a similar situation?

We as human beings can look at the conditions of lack and limitation and see the beauty beyond them. Loss or lack might be a current fact for those we are serving or even for ourselves, but it is *never* a fixed state of being. It is never our spiritual truth.

Emma Curtis Hopkins, a New Thought teacher of the early 1900s wrote, "If a starving child spent even a few minutes imagining someone giving her food, food would find its way to her."

We knew very little about how to host an event like this, or what type of operative framework a food drive would require. We knew we needed all the help we could get. We decided to make sure we were covered, spiritually, first. It turns out that the whole endeavor requires quite a bit of money to be paid up front, namely for the hundreds of pounds of bulk foods that need to be packaged. We had never raised money before for a project outside of the regular support of our center.

Things were rough in Central Florida during the 2007-2009 recession, so for the time being, we decided to package food for local food banks instead of for Tanzania. We envisioned what we wanted to experience, how we wanted to feel about it during, and afterward, and generally how things would go. How could we look at raising money in a way that was fun, creative, and inspiring, so others would want to be a part of the action? Instead of feeling sorry for those without, how could we uplift them in a way that empowers us all? And perhaps most importantly, where could we hold such an event?

We got into the feeling of what it would mean to us and to those who were going to receive those meals.

We drew from a deeper place within us for our creation. It made all the difference. After wrapping our minds around the idea of what we wanted to create, ideas came to us about who to contact for the other necessary items needed for the event. One by one, solutions came to the forefront. Our way was made easy. We were being divinely led through the fog. Each one of us had to ask ourselves:

What can I do to make this an exceptional experience?

What doubts, fears, or reservations do I have that could get in the way of our community event?

We had to admit whatever they were so they could be addressed. Certain individuals had to release their doubts about where we were going to get the money. As each person said their part, others added, "You know, I could have said that as well." We skillfully covered every angle as we followed Spirit's lead and acted together as one mind. Once we sufficiently identified what our primary blocks and hesitations were, we could more clearly separate them from the greater Truth.

In further preparation, we decided it was best for us to conduct a group visioning session. We asked a carefully considered list of our most important questions, and listened for answers:

VISIONING SESSION

What does Spirit want to express or experience through and as us in the way of our expression, our path, our relationships, our physical location or dwelling, our health, our wealth?

What does that look like and feel like?

What strengths do I bring to the situation?

What do I need to release so this can happen?

What do I need to embrace?

Is there anything else I need to know?

We ended up using this visioning process for all three of the packaging events we organized for The Outreach Program that year.

The second one was held in Maitland, Florida (relatively close to Orlando) under a large, donated tent in the parking lot of the Qdoba Mexican Grill. Packaging required putting together specific measurements of bulk rice, beans, flavorings, and vitamins to make a healthy, complete meal. The recipe was originally designed for malnourished children in Africa, whose dietary needs are much different than ours. Today, we would use this food for those needing nutrition in our own city.

In the visioning process, we saw a sunny day. Even though we would be packing the food inside a very large tent, completed boxes waiting for pickup needed to be stacked outside. It could not rain.

As we got closer to our big day, questions continued to surface about what we were going to do if it rained. "What is Plan B?" we were asked over and over. It was close to December when the area typically gets more precipitation. Our team affirmed over and over again: "There is no Plan B. It's going to be a sunny day. It's going to be perfect. It's going to be a great day for packaging food. It is already a success." That is how we answered the question and how we reinforced the *mental image* we intended to project.

The day arrived, and it was sunny. Maybe it was always going to be, regardless of what we'd done. It no longer mattered, because we got what we needed. That's an example of what's possible. It could have been a catastrophe, but I believe we would have been directed otherwise, and a backup location would have been available to us. Since we were getting no such information, we stood our ground. Our intention was genuine. Everything was in place and we were ready to go. The goal was achieved.

Within 18 months, our small and mighty community, along with a wonderful team of dedicated volunteers, raised nearly $28,000 and packaged 100,000 meals for our local food banks throughout those three events. We were most grateful, not only for what we were able to share with our community but for the opportunity to work together as a cohesive team with a beautiful purpose. We grew and expanded spiritually in tremendous ways from those experiences. And for many of us, including myself, it reaffirmed the efficacy of the visioning process in achieving a big-picture goal.

About a year later, myself and two ministers from CSL's Global Service's Ministries set up an organization-wide food packaging event at Denver's Mile High Church, along with another large one at our Youth Camp that year. It was inspiring to be a part of the planning and implantation of packaging over 130,000 meals for Africa. It was an honor and privilege to see people, including our youth, from centers across the nation come together and serve Africa, as one.

INTENTIONS

Getting people fed physically and having everyone involved fed emotionally, socially and spiritually.

Our focus was on community building and teamwork within our own organization.

Applying our spiritual practices—giving of our time, talent, and treasure.

Seeing past conditions to Universal Truths—Abundance is our true nature.

Developing our own spiritual maturity thus deepening our relationship with Spirit.

DEMONSTRATION

Central Florida Center for Spiritual Living raised $28,000 and prepared 100,000 meals to donate to the Second Harvest Food Bank in Florida.

Raised $38,000 and prepared 130,000 meals as our greater Centers for Spiritual Living organization for Tanzania.

Chapter Thirteen: The Great Blue Heron

"Remember this: The Truth, when it arrives, is always different from what we thought it would be. If we imagine that we already know the truth, that imagination is based on old and habitual ideas. But the truth is always something entirely new to the mind; therefore, we cannot know what a new day is like before we experience it, we cannot think accurately about a new truth until we first live it."

— Vernon Howard, *Psycho-Pictography*

I was fortunate enough to be able to purchase my first piece of property from a couple of my closest friends. They pulled out all the stops to help make it happen. It was a beautiful condo in Lawrenceville, Georgia, just outside of Atlanta—a corner unit, with a lovely private patio, facing a rather large pond. It was so liberating to finally have a place of my very own. I had made great strides during the previous couple of years of my singlehood, both mentally and emotionally. Now, it was time to take on a challenge I'd longed for since my divorce: A new, beautiful place I could call my own. Somewhere steady and welcoming that my children could visit, stay, and look forward to returning to. It was a very special spot. I still think about it to this day.

In the early morning hours as I prepared for work, I was facing a window in view of the pond when something caught my eye: a gorgeous blue bird stoically perched at the edge of the water. He stood motionless, seemingly studying the water, hopeful for his daily catch, exuding an awareness of everything that was going on around him. I saw him again the next morning, and every morning after that. With remarkable consistency, he made his way back to the pond every single day, eloquently watching and waiting for just the right moment, clear or cloudy, rain or shine.

After a few weeks of this, observing him became a part of my own daily routine. I would jump out of bed to greet him. Sometimes just for a moment, sometimes for many moments. And there we would faithfully rest, together, in silent and astute awareness. It reassured me to have such a constant reminder of my connection with nature. I cherished every moment I was able to spend with him. The simple act of noticing him seemed to have a powerfully calming effect on me. This practice was always one of the best ways to start my day.

After a couple of years at the condo, I met John, remarried, and moved to Orlando. I forgot all about the bird.

Time passed, and I would see an occasional heron, here and there, and remember my blue friend in Lawrenceville. There was just something truly striking about these mighty, nimble, sapient birds. My memories of Georgia brought me so much joy and comfort. And before I knew it, Great Blue Herons (and their sister, the Great White Egret) started showing up for me in the most incredibly surprising ways. I would see them on my daily walks. Sometimes, they crossed my path while I was driving. Once, one flew alongside me while I drove back home from dropping Liz off at the airport after she had come to visit us at our home in Orlando. I took this as confirmation of a successful visit! I loved how this was evolving. In the language of totems, these birds became my spirit animal. I couldn't wait to go for my morning walks in anticipation of how I might witness Spirit showing up for me through my surroundings.

The renewal of my appreciation for them extended into a newfound connection to owls and hawks, as well. Two other very wise and powerful birds. Like the heron, they too became my touchstone to the Infinite world. To this day, whenever I see one, I think of Spirit, knowing we are making contact.

The Cover of I Can Do This Thing Called Life: And So Can You!

Before my relationship with birds had been established, I was working on my first book, *I Can Do This Thing Called Life and So Can You!*, and on the lookout for something eye-catching to put on the cover. The book wasn't finished, but I was hopeful that finding my cover, something that captured the essence of the words I had so far, would help it all come together.

On one amazingly beautiful morning that fall, I was canoeing down the Wekiva River with my sister-in-law, Joby. She shares my passion for nature. The river belonged to us that day. No one else was around. We savored every precious moment. Little did we know, this was about to become a once-in-a-lifetime adventure. We had no idea of what lay ahead.

After we had paddled for about twenty minutes in blissful silence, I noticed something odd up ahead, off to the left. I pointed it out to Joby. We both watched with suspicion and curiosity as we got closer.

A few moments later, it became clear. It was a ten-foot-long alligator outstretched on a life-sized log, basking in the sun. I had a quick reaction of, "Should we be afraid?" and an equally quick—and unequivocal—response to my own question, "No."

Joby seemed to agree with me. She was already leaning in to take pictures. As she and I paddled cautiously by the log and its occupant, we studied the gator in amazement. Likewise, the gator's eyes never left us. The Universe was looking at Itself through each set of eyes. It was a powerful moment.

In the same way that seeing the log up close brought the alligator into sharp focus for Joby and me, seeing the alligator up close brought *I Can Do This Thing Called Life: and So Can You!* into sharp focus for me. Wow! A picture really is worth a thousand words— even several thousand. Here was this stupendous reptilian creature, a survivor of an ancient species that has been successfully adapting to an ever-changing world for millions of years, yet has remained, in its essence, the very same as it has always been since the beginning of its time. In my search for the perfect cover art for my book, Spirit delivered to me: A living, breathing, full-color image of perfection.

The message of spiritual significance flooded into my mind without effort. Alligators have a determined sense of survival, and (contrary to popular myth) they are excellent mothers. They also possess a spellbinding power and presence. They are patient. They only eat when they are hungry, and when they do, they digest their nutrients slowly, taking every bit of it in. They see and know everything that is going on around them, even when hidden beneath the surface of murky water.

In short, this magnificent creature is the embodiment of the core teaching that I wanted this book to convey: Every one of us is strong, powerful, resilient, adaptable, and compelling, even if we don't think we are. We are all a survivor of something that could've taken us out, had we not been adaptable even in the face of unspeakable challenges, and stacked odds, we have succeeded in becoming the amazing, incredible beings that we are. Each one of us has our own unique path to follow, and our true happiness depends on finding that path—the road less traveled with our name on it. My hope was that this book could offer signposts along the way and serve as a reminder of this.

It was my hope that the timeless symbolism of the alligator would speak to my readers and remind them of their right to be here, and to be proud of who they were: an ancient being in the making here to have an incredible adventure. That was the hope. In reality, to those who had not shared such a positive and enlightening experience with a colloquially dangerous creature, the concept was quite a big leap. While it did ultimately inspire me to complete my very first book and get it to print, and the publisher went along with my wishes, the public's reactions surprised me. They couldn't get behind the idea that a reptile, looking so prehistoric with such a reputation as the alligator, could possibly be put in the same conversation as spirituality. I guess that's what spending 26 years in Florida's nature will get you. So it was first published with the alligator cover, but as time went along and the public's feedback started coming in, it was clear that a new cover was in order. At that time, it was more fitting to have the book republished with a Great Blue Heron. Ultimately, the Alligator gave me the perfect end result plus a hair-raising adventure in the wild with my sister-in-law, and eventually led me back to the totem that has become even more meaningful to me throughout my spiritual journey. It definitely served a great purpose.

The Cover of Energize Your Creative Super Powers, 7 Ways to Spiritual Fitness

Years after my first book had made it to the shelves, I began working on my second. This time, a workbook called *Energize Your Creative Super Powers, 7 Ways to Spiritual*

Fitness. Once again, I found myself in a similar position, in search of a cover. One gorgeous, warm day, I'd been invited out to lunch with some friends in the small town of Eustis, on the outskirts of Orlando. While traversing through the heart of the downtown area, I noticed a huge water fountain. I started towards it to get a better look, when I recognized that in the middle of the basin, there was a larger than life-like metal sculpture of a Great Blue Heron. Of course, I had to get a picture. Through some detective work, I managed to find out who the sculptor was. Doug Hays: a self-taught, local artist. He gave me permission to use the picture if I provided him with a copy of my book. In a symbiotic way, the picture of his sculpture reignited the fire I needed to complete it.

Doug described his artistic process this way:

I have always been intrigued by anything transformed by fire; fire is what drew me to working metal. The excitement of a burning forge and hammering hot iron drew my attention and hooked me immediately. Being rooted in the venerable blacksmithing tradition, I still use my hammer and anvil daily, but I also use modern power tools and computer-controlled machinery. I taught myself how to sculpt metal through reading books and experimentation. Along the way, I learned how to combine ancient and modern techniques. I enjoy the challenge of bringing life to steel, imparting a feeling of motion and expression to an unyielding and heavy material. What has developed is an intuitive physical process of heating, hammering, bending, welding, and grinding that produces organic and rhythmic sculptures from hard iron. Over the last twelve years, I have focused on public art. I'm proud to have placed sculptures in some of the cities here in Florida. I believe that art enriches all of our lives and brings us together. It offers cultural identity and civic pride. I enjoy the creative process from conception to installation.

INTENTION

I needed inspiration. Being a visual person, the idea came to me to find a picture for my cover. Not having any ideas, I decided both times that the idea for the cover would find me. I would recognize them when I saw them.

AFFIRMATION

Universe, I now demonstrate the perfect cover for my book.

DEMONSTRATION

Lovely pictures of Great Blue Herons as covers for my books which have great meaning for me. In the wild, they represent Spirit to me. Looking at them always brings a smile to my face because my intention was heard and the perfect result showed up.

Chapter Fourteen: A Spiritual Bookstore

"Every blade of grass has its Angel that bends over it and whispers, 'Grow, grow.'"

— The Talmud

"There are no happier people on this planet than those who decide that they want something, define what they want, get hold of the feeling of it even before its manifestation and then joyously watch the unfolding as, piece by piece by piece, it begins to unfold. That's the feeling of your hands in the clay."

— Esther Hicks/Abraham

We were elated to learn that the Centers for Spiritual Living Conference was being held in Orlando. The planning committee asked us if we would create a bookstore for the occasion, which would feature an assortment of chosen books and music from our favorite authors and artists all over the country.

This was no small feat. Our Center was still relatively small at the time in comparison to others that had hosted the Conference in the past few years. The Conference was set to last a full week. I hesitated as I approached our people with the proposition. To my surprise and delight, they said yes! They were just as excited about the opportunity as I was. Even though I felt tremendous pressure to lead this group endeavor in an area where I had no prior experience, I was feeling pretty optimistic. I love books! Colleagues from all over the country would be attending. I also knew this was an opportunity for our people to connect with people from all over the world. This was going to be exciting.

To help calm my nerves, I spent more time than usual on my spiritual practices. I needed all the support I could get!

The bookstore exceeded my wildest expectations. We had jewelry, cards, framed photography, CDs, audiobooks, and of course, inspirational books. I was even able to proudly add my first book to the collection. Even with all of the hard work we'd put into the lead-up, our entire group was able and eager to extend warm, thoughtful hospitality to the visiting crowds throughout the week. We created a happy place together for hundreds of others to enjoy along with us. I was so proud of the community of volunteers who stepped up and chose to do such a great job creating a lovely experience on such short notice. A few of our technologically savvy members created a financial program to track the sales transactions for the week. By the time the conference came to a close, we'd brought in more money than we'd projected. Our team was on it! It was a huge success.

MY IDEAL DAY...

...is filled with Me—the real ME takes over boldly, confidently. I am sure of myself. I wake up well-rested, energized, inspired and ready to go. I commit to staying in my director position, letting others step up and get involved, knowing every last detail is handled. The pieces of the grand puzzle come together, beautifully fitting in their proper place, piece by piece. We have everything we need and beyond, including an accounting system to track every detail of our fiscal responsibility. I feel confident we are ready for action and fully capable of doing it all!

The love and presence that each person brings to this experience is astounding, including my own, and everything that happens from here on out is testimony to our great love, dedication, commitment, and work—radical love and support we give ourselves and each other. Setting distractions and detours aside, we are directed, clear, focused, insistent on the Truth that we are already a success.

The truth is that we are loved, supported, cared for, guided, provided for, inspired and transformed. Our creative, loving center/community gives birth to this magnificent collaboration of art, expression and music. Incredibly talented and gifted individuals bring their best to the party.

I am so grateful for the enthusiasm, loving kindness, energy, and powerful presence of all involved. Goods are purchased and circulate throughout the world, finding their way to those that need upliftment. By the end of the week, people want to know how they can share all of this goodness with their loved ones.

This bookstore is wildly successful and takes all to new heights of pleasure and experience, opening doors where doors were not possible before, shedding light on dark places, opening up more ideas for collaboration and fun.

MY IDEAL DAY...

...is filled with all of the magnificence, beauty and wonder of YOU, Great Spirit! Today, YOU guide me in putting all the finishing touches in place. I feel good about being ready and my/our team moves into action together. This is the day we have been

waiting for. We have been preparing for this as a community. The very highest and best comes out of us all. Everyone is touched by their participation in it. Everyone that brought something to the table has been elevated energetically and taken to another level before we even begin. We are blessed beyond measure – flying high this entire week and beyond. We have the capacity to stay strong and firm in mind about the Truth, knowing we have plenty of volunteers to serve all week long. We experience the greatest success ever in our lives, which includes new heights of consciousness/expansion like we never felt before.

The truth is we are carried through this week and beyond. We are living the charmed life now, the only life there is, the life of Spirit.

Thank you, Divine, Infinite Partner in me for blessing me with this project and taking my consciousness to new heights of appreciation and love. I am, we are, so blessed.

AFFIRMATIONS

Thank you for an exquisitely run bookstore and the magic of YOU bringing together all the talents, gifts and expertise we may need. It is a WOW experience, (WOW was the name of the conference)!

Thanks for giving me the courage to take on this project. All the pieces, parts and players come together now with ease, joy and fun, giving our community a chance to play and work together to create something fabulous.

The Center for Spiritual Living convention in Orlando is a culmination of the best possibilities of everyone involved. This is a conference to remember – a party sponsored by heaven ITself. Prosperity and goodness flow like fine wine. We drink generously from the fountain of Life!

Our flow expands. We enjoy the lavish attention we receive from the Universe. We humbly serve and are exquisitely provided for. This is the best bookstore ever! Thank you for this amazing experience!

MIND TREATMENT | FEBRUARY 4TH, 2017

There is One Magnificent Power and Presence in the Universe that reigns supreme over all.

I am one with the Infinite Spirit that creates worlds and that created me. I am Invincible Spirit acting through and as me.

Source provides for me abundantly, to the last detail, everything I could possibly need or want to live the richest life possible. I stand on top of the mountain with my arms open wide in adoration of the Perfection of all that is. I stand on the mountain top and see from the highest heights the Supreme Truth of All.

This week, everything demonstrates to perfection, for us, personally, for our bookstore and for the entire convention. I am so appreciative of all that is mine and enjoy my spirit soaring.

I release this treatment now, knowing my perfection and allowing Spirit the greatest possible experience in me—living in, as and through me always.

And so it is!

INTENTION

Creating a fully functioning bookstore for the conference with five months' notice.

DEMONSTRATION

A successful convention and bookstore.

Chapter Fifteen: 20th Anniversary

"...it is the divinity of man in expression; and when we learn to convert human passion into divine love, to transmute the lower into the higher, we shall have with us a power of attraction against which nothing can stand."

— Ernest Holmes, *The Creative Mind*

"All things are waiting to be looked upon by us as they really are."

— Emma Curtis Hopkins

At the dawn of the new year in 2014, John and I were approaching a milestone of twenty years in service to the Central Florida Center for Spiritual Living. We stopped to reflect on all we had accomplished. We took time to remember and appreciate the thousands of people we'd had a chance to get to know and connect with along the way. We gave thanks to as many of the individuals we'd been able to help toward spiritual growth and healing as we could. We declared our appreciation for all of the beautiful friends and partnerships that had blossomed under our roof. It had been two decades of non-stop work, and on the other side of it the only thing I felt was tremendous gratitude. It took many committed, generous souls to get us this far. Through the gifts of their time, talent, money, and love, they all played an integral part in what it'd taken to keep a community going for so long. Their gifts allowed us to make these invaluable teachings available to as many people as possible. It's impossible to name all who were responsible for us being here today. We are so grateful for each and every one of them. We all grew tremendously from our experiences of working together.

Now, it was time to celebrate! Immersed in the process, year after year, we hadn't even considered any of the other milestones along the way. Five, ten, and fifteen years had all passed us by without much thought. The Universe started the celebration by reminding us that we were long overdue. Now the time seemed right. We declared a huge, blowout party was in order, and the Universe got right to work.

A few years ago, we attended a member's wedding reception at the Florida Federation of Garden Clubs. It was a breathtaking setting with a large outdoor patio and lively, sprawling gardens. I had filed this wonderful venue in my mind for future possibilities. Once we started the planning process for our celebration, it was my first choice for the potential location, and I had to check it out. I met up with the property's manager,

Dawn, who delighted me with the news that it would be available for the dates we had in mind. But not only that—she let me know that the space was actually going to be completely unoccupied on Sunday mornings for the foreseeable future. When she saw the look on my face, she knew we were thinking the same thing. This would be a perfect place for our group to meet regularly. One thing led to another, and the next thing I knew, we were signing contracts, all the while reveling in yet another unexpected gift from the Divine. It was mid-December, and I couldn't help but consider this an early holiday present.

The story behind all this is that we never had a building of our own. I have often been grateful for not owning one during the rougher Florida hurricane seasons. It was nice not having the responsibility of a building to maintain so we could invest even more of our time and focus on our work. There were plenty of beautiful places to meet in Orlando. In the mid-90s to the early 2000s, we were primarily at the Maitland Civic Center, which was also a beautiful setting, with a view of a large fountain in the middle of Lake Lily. Because it was used for art festivals as well, there were some weekends when we did not have access to it. On those Sundays, we chose to go to a park, have a short service, and picnic afterward.

One of the parks that we used back then was Meade Gardens, which is right next to the Florida Federation of Garden Clubs. In fact, on our first Sunday meeting at the Garden Club, I had a view of the very pavilion we'd used back then from where I happened to be sitting in the front row. Meade Gardens also holds memories of workshops with Dr. Jane Claypool, author of *Wise Women Don't Worry, Wise Women Don't Sing the Blues*, and Carol Adrienne, who co-authored with James Redfield *The Celestine Prophecy, An Experiential Guide*.

At their beautiful outdoor amphitheater, we held the memorial for Ray Eisenmenger, our Assistant Minister, who was my right hand in the early years, and two of our dearly-loved practitioners, Carol and Taylor, along with other members and friends. This garden, adjacent to our new place, was sacred ground to us. It held some of our roots, bringing back memories of experiences long forgotten.

Almost twenty years later, we'd come full circle. It was so gratifying, and so immensely pleasurable to connect these dots and be able to witness the greater Reality that had come into being. We had grown so much since then. We were a completely different community and organization than the one who'd dreamed of being where we are today, all those years ago.

The Anniversary turned out to be quite a party. Catering was covered by a former member, there were unique non-alcoholic cocktails (or mocktails), we enjoyed live entertainment from our favorite musicians and artists, and another member, an avid gardener, decorated the room with greenery from her garden and home. We were immensely grateful. Delicious foods presented in creative and unusual ways, the enjoyment of friends and family, talks, lively music, and dancing brought big smiles to our faces. Everything was done with great thought and love. To top it off, we had Kenn Gordon, our spiritual leader at the time, flown in from Canada for the festivities. It was a night to remember.

Thank you, Universe, for the perfect unfoldment of a divine plan. I am so grateful! I'd say that You have no idea how much this journey has meant to me, but I know that You do.

INTENTION

Find a special place to host our 20 years celebration of being

Central Florida Center for Spiritual Living

IDEAL DAY

Our center flourishes like never before. We are a true center of inspiration, wisdom and love, teaching Universal Principles to all who are ready. Our spiritual leadership includes absolutely wonderful people who are in alignment with us and happy to create together. A new day is born, our vision is clear, and it is now fulfilled. Our dreams are realized. Huge breakthroughs put us on a new and exciting course, taking everyone along for the ride.

IDEAL DAY | DECEMBER 7TH, 2014

Looking out the window to the gardens, as I had on our first Sunday, I recognized a pavilion in the near distance where we had picnics in our early years.

Today, we celebrate having our first Sunday in our new home at the Garden Club. It is such a healing place—a room with lots of windows to connect us to the beautiful gardens that surround it. It is so amazing that we demonstrated this sacred space in the middle of the hustle and bustle of the city—a place that feeds the soul without having to say a word.

Thank you for a special Sunday! All who can be healed, blessed and prospered find their way to us easily and effortlessly. Our coming together is a dynamic exchange of energy and love for which we are supported beautifully in all ways. We are encouraged to keep on keeping on!

Thank YOU, Universe, for showing us the way to support ourselves more greatly along with this beautiful center.

VISIONING SESSION WITH THE TEAM

What is Spirit's idea of Itself as our 20th Anniversary Celebration?

Homecoming, outreach to past members and visitors, coming together, lovefest, bonding, uniting of CFCSL with the community at large, playful, involves friends, lots of people from other CSL centers in the Southeast Region, huge celebration, no pressure celebration, no expectation from the guests, mutual gifts to the community and from the community.

What does it taste like, feel like, smell like?

Opulence, tasteful, feels like friends coming together, forgotten friends partake, important for us, brings us together, raises our image, dressy, musical, New Thought and Metaphysical music, happy, festive, intelligent, safe, joyous, bright, silver & white, streamers, light, circular and open, balloons, a recommitment, a restatement of what CFCSL is, party-like, Spirit-networking.

What must I become in order for that vision to be fulfilled?

Present, focused, allowing, trusting, listening, open, free, available, set the tone, set the stage visually to build the celebration upon, less shy, more a part of the community, open to suggestions, approach people, courageous, know the idea is supported, be a leader.

What must I release in order for that vision to be fulfilled?

The idea that it has to be a lot of work or that there won't be enough help/support/resources, fear of criticism, rejection, judgment, making it happen, any doubt that a huge affair can happen, any and all fear, sense of lack, money or location.

What must I embrace in order to embody the vision?

Loving support from everyone, celebration, delegating, cooperation, collaboration, planning, that this is a divine idea that has life to it, energizes and gives to us versus taking away from us, my extroverted side, my sameness, like-mindedness.

Is there anything else to be known at this time?

It's already done in Universal Mind and plays out for our enjoyment and pleasure. It is right to celebrate all of our efforts and who we are, we have a right to be proud. This event serves the greater good of us all and puts us on the map.

OMG! - APRIL 15TH, 2015

OMG! You are amazing...incredible what You can pull off. You magnificently demonstrated a way to pay every financial obligation for the 20th, above and beyond our regular income, including seed money for new experiences. $12,000 minimum was achieved. It was the most perfect evening event ever. I enjoyed myself thoroughly and so did everyone else. I secretly knew You planned the whole party for me. I was the one who knew the real demonstration...the whole story...who we had become as a community, who I had become because of my work, who John had become because of this center. You not only presented perfection that night and weekend, (everyone left happy and elated), You found creative ways to fund it all. I am enamored by You and Your love for me, for us all!

Thank You! Thank You! I love you so much and trust You forever!

DEMONSTRATION

Raised $10,000, had 100 attendees, Successful Celebration of 20 years together

and New Sunday Space

Section III

The Encore

Chapter Sixteen: Leaving the Nest

"As soon as you are certain that whatever has come surging over your life can't hurt you at all, the perfect condition shows forth out of that Substance, and things come out right."

— Emma Curtis Hopkins

"It's human nature to wish to make others do what we think they should be doing. It's divine to see that their way is their true way.

...As we give all people absolute freedom in our minds, they will do the right things."

— Emma Curtis Hopkins

"For once you have tasted flight, you will forever walk the earth with your eyes turned skyward, for there you have been, and there you will always long to return."

— Leonardo da Vinci

John and I have had the pleasure of raising a child from birth to adulthood, together. When Joseph was born, we lived in a suburb of Altamonte Springs along the northwestern border of Orlando, in a neighborhood filled with other families. He went to school with a handful of the kids in our area and became close friends with them over the course of his childhood and adolescence. Throughout the years, we and the other parents had a front-row seat to their physical, social, emotional, and intellectual transformation from expressive, creative, and curious young spirits to amazing, accomplished, independent adults.

Raising a child is no easy task, but under the right conditions, it is rewarding beyond belief. Although Joseph was not my first taste of motherhood, a lot of the experience of raising him was uncharted territory for me. Having been unable to raise my eldest two full-time, I was grateful to have another chance to experience all of the parts of the journey.

Of course, much of the process was familiar. Just like Nic and Elizabeth, he was curious, bright, and beautiful. And, as all pure spirits do, he knew exactly who he was, and what he was made of. He knew what he wanted in life from a very young age, seemingly born with a strong internal motivation to get it, as if he had emerged from the ether with a mission, an assignment, and a due date. He ended up being quite the teacher for us.

Because John and I were older parents, we had the unique advantage, which many of our peers had to do without, of being more aware. Because of the extensive work we'd both done in our own personal lives, we were far more spiritually aware than either of us had been in our 20s or 30s. In addition to that, we'd been through the mill. We had years—decades—of experiences and challenges of varying degrees that shaped and refined us. When you've spent years working on your own personal development, you begin to notice an interesting phenomenon: the more you strive to understand, nourish, and support yourself, the deeper your capacity to care for and nurture others—the more unconditional, powerful, and healing your love becomes. You begin to reveal an ever-expanding appreciation for all beings coming from God, and this understanding gradually makes its way to the forefront of your mind. Your actions progressively stem from a commitment to love others, especially children, to the best of your ability.

Spiritual work also helps us to recognize all beings as equals, from the moment they arrive in this physical world to the moment they leave. How can you not pay special attention to these beings fresh from the other side, direct from the immaterial spiritual world? Without an ounce of the baggage or limiting beliefs we may wish we'd never claimed along the way, these spirits are free. In my philosophy, it stands to reason that they have a unique perspective and insight worthy of paying attention to. It even crosses my mind when I notice a newborn staring off into the corner of a room. What...or who...do they see that we can't? And what really *is* imagination? A defining aspect of the child's experience that adults can so easily write off as simple, cute, or nonsensical, it somehow feels riddled with unanswered truths about our mind's power. Do we even remember what it feels like to be able to create and live in a fully immersive world, stemming entirely from our own choice and intention? Children are more our teachers than we are theirs.

Thank God our years of experience in the world and studies in human development gave us tools that would prove useful in our interactions together. Being present, listening, processing emotions, resolving conflicts, practicing affirmations, and staying positive were skills we are grateful to have been able to demonstrate and share with him. We wanted to know what he thought about things. We were there to support what he wanted to do. We were committed to helping him learn how to help himself. Our desire was to model a creative, loving, intentional way of being. Even though it was a workout, our life was rich and rewarding in so many ways. If I could do it over again, I wouldn't change much.

One day while walking up to our favorite Italian restaurant in Wekiva Springs for pizza, Joseph, who was about 4 at the time, veered off to look in the window of a local karate dojo which was right next to it. He peered into the window and headed for the door, determined to find out more. I stopped him and promised we would look into it another time. Later that week, we signed him up for a 12-month program, which he loved. Mr. Zamboni was his main instructor. He learned self-respect, self-control, patience, and focus, and as an added bonus, it was the perfect way for him to channel his tremendous amount of energy and blow off some steam! Naturally, we kept taking him. By the time he was ten years old, he'd earned his 3rd degree black belt.

After about six years of that, he was ready to try out a team sport. He'd always been a strong swimmer—you have to be when you live in Florida! Lake Brantley High School had a fabulous Olympic-size swimming pool, and he knew some of the kids on their swim team for the younger age group. It seemed like the logical next step.

Middle school can be such a huge transition, for parent and child. One day they're playing with legos and then, rather abruptly, they're learning about sex and drugs. With an hour-and-a-half-long practice, three nights a week, swimming turned out to be a great way for him to get his mental and physical health in shape and for me to work on my first book. I sat in the bleachers writing while I watched these young swimmers gliding through the water with grace and ease. Watching them inspired me and cleared my head to write more effectively.

After a year and a half, he intuitively knew he was done with swimming. Though swimming was a team sport, he wanted to work more closely with a group whose individual performances were intrinsically connected to a result they earned together.

He joined the middle school band, and by the time high school years were in full swing, Joseph and most of his closest friends were in the marching band. He loved music and did quite well on the saxophone. He continued to practice and play increasingly ambitious songs with his friends for several years. Mrs. Berry, the high school music director, had been there for years. Everyone knew who she was. She was strict, but she knew how to get the members to put on quite a show. They always did well in state-wide competitions. I loved going to the football games to see their choreographed marches and listen to their amazing music. It was incredible to see their dance moves while at the same time producing this powerful music.

He'd also joined the rowing team in middle school and managed to keep up with it throughout his time at Lake Brantley, in addition to band and being an excellent student. Rowing became his life. I never knew teenagers to jump out of bed at the crack of dawn just to practice or travel to a meet. Joseph and his teammates loved being in the boat on the water together. They learned to work together with precision and confidence. Every available moment was focused on crew or practice. He shared his heart and soul with it. First, he became the captain of the junior team. Then, captain of the varsity team.

It was the best of both worlds for him. Not only was it a team sport that centered on synchronized movements and effective communication, but it also relied on the physical and mental fortitude of every individual. No one could drop the ball, or shift the weight of their load, even for a second, without risking the efforts of the entire team. His experience with this crew bolstered his mental and physical endurance, perseverance, mindfulness, and self-esteem.

Time flies under such conditions. The years certainly did. One minute I was teaching him how to walk, and then all of a sudden, it was time for him to leave the nest. I had no idea how to prepare myself for the day Joseph would leave for college, much less how to help him leave in the best way possible. Again, this was uncharted territory. Thankfully, in Nic and Liz's case, their father and stepmom were able to give them some worthy guidance.

We clung to the words of Joseph's middle school guidance counselor for faith: "Any student in the gifted program is eligible for scholarships from the big schools."

Whether it was true or not, I returned to those words whenever a worry crossed my mind. I didn't know what else to do. We weren't exactly in a position to pay for 4 years of college out of pocket, and we didn't want that to be the only thing standing in his way. He had dreams of the Ivy League, the big Northeastern Universities, Vanderbilt, nothing that was local, nowhere that was Florida. John and I were working for a religious non-profit, which is dependent on donations, in a transient area of the country, so there was little leftover to put away for his education. As graduation day approached like a bullet train, my uncertainty increased by the moment. While I didn't have the time to logistically ensure a way for it to take place (i.e. come up with $165,000, give or take), I decided to lean into my spiritual practices to begin solidifying what we hoped for him to experience.

PART OF AN IDEAL DAY

Two years prior to graduation

We take our power back and step fully into the most exciting time of our lives. Everything needed, necessary and beyond, is ours now – right here, available to us to make this the best possible life for us all. We all, being directed by the Infinite Intelligence of Life within us, KNOW WHAT TO DO, know what our part is, see our way, believe and know the absolute best is underway and already completed in the mind of God. Today, we thoroughly enjoy having mastered this situation regarding Joseph's future and seeing how ideal and perfect things can be.

We stand in Wonder and Awe of YOU, knowing a most ideal situation for Joseph transpires. Something wonderful and beautiful that feeds him and allows him to flourish occurs. Next steps and phases that are comfortable and pleasurable for him and take him where he wants to go. At the same time, they expand and entice him to live his genius and be his real, genuine self.

Being a top student, Joseph applied to schools on the merit of his academics. To our dismay, he evidently had a lot of competition. He didn't make it into most of the schools that judged applicants primarily on their grades, but he didn't seem too discouraged; he knew he had more than one path forward.

You might have noticed a common theme amongst Joseph's extracurriculars of choice: he loves being active and being with others. Because he'd earned captain of his varsity rowing team, his participation in rowing became another card to play. Even with his original plan to go for academics, crew was never off the table. He knew he'd want to keep doing it in the future, regardless of anything else.

He informed us that he'd been looking into the University of Washington. UW has one of the best crew teams in the country. We'd all watched a documentary together a few years back called *Boys in the Boat*, which was based on the book by Daniel James Brown. It's a story about nine young UW students and their quest for a gold medal at the 1936 Berlin Olympics. A dramatic movie was released in 2023 based on the same source material.

His exact words were, "I kind of want to just apply there for the fun of it."

By that, he meant that the school was out of state and beyond too expensive for what we thought we could manage. But also it meant, he wasn't worried about the result. He was just keeping an open mind. What could it hurt?

As the applications went out, and the response letters came back in, the one and only school he immediately got accepted to was the University of Washington. The one he'd applied to for fun.

During his decision-making process, he was in communication with the crew coach at UW and was invited to try out for them in the Fall. His stats were comparable to what they were looking for. This would also grant him a small scholarship to help offset the out-of-state cost.

Once he officially made the decision that he was going to go to school there, he figured he'd better mention his very flat feet to the coach. His coach responded, "Well, you're going to have to run excessively, so go get yourself some good orthotics, and get yourself out here."

Running had always been difficult for him, and learning it would be a huge part of his training made him doubt his choice. He was still on the waitlist for Vanderbilt. He had options. But within what couldn't have been more than a minute or two, in a true testament to the human spirit and his own maturity, he looked at me with a smile and said, "Well, I guess I'm going to have to accept this challenge."

I couldn't help but smile. To this day, I am inspired by his tenacity. He followed up with the coach to ask what kind of training he should be expecting. He likened it to that of a Navy Seal."

No one can accuse the Universe of lacking a sense of humor. The stakes were getting higher by the minute. We made an appointment with the podiatrist. In private, Joseph admitted to me that he had some serious doubts about his feet's ability to withstand such rigorous training.

The lead-up to the appointment was a challenging time for me as well. *Should I be encouraging him in this direction? What if it leads to permanent injury?* I shared Joseph's concern and uncertainty in the matter, especially given the diagnosis we'd been given previously, but I was vigilant to stop myself whenever I started questioning things. NO! There is no need to fear.

We wouldn't be led this way so strongly without there being a path for us to walk on. We are working with Intelligence, and IT works intelligently. We are working with IT intelligently. We just have to keep going.

The day finally came. We were all anxiously anticipating the doctor's opinion. What would he say? Would he think we were crazy for even trying? Could anything he said even stop us from continuing? Really, we just needed the orthotics. We could worry about the next steps when we got there.

On day one, X-rays were taken. The doctor, Joseph, and I all stared at their images in silence. From my non-professional eye, they looked perfect. I had been expecting some blatant abnormality. Sure, they were flat, but the bones were beautifully spaced within each other. Nothing looking too crowded or dangerous. The podiatrist agreed. He said he couldn't see anything that would prevent him from running perfectly with orthotics. And for extra measure, he assured us that he saw nothing that would indicate a need for future surgery.

We both could have cried. I stood up and thanked the specialist profusely, and with that, our family was freed from the discord that had previously festered within us in the lead-up to this joyous moment. We knew what goals needed to be met to qualify, and now he had the confidence in his ability to achieve them.

We drove out of the clinic's parking lot with so much giddiness that we could not stop ourselves from reveling in the news the whole way home. Sometimes a new perspective is necessary. We hold onto so much unsorted energetic weight when we don't know where to put it. It prevents us from soaring. If we can manage to free ourselves up with a wider perspective, even if it's just a little bit wider, we can see the way more clearly and be privy to more options of what is possible.

His love for crew led to him trying out for the best crew team in the United States. Washington, here we come! But first, graduation. He ended up ranking 3rd in his class of six hundred seniors. He was nominated to give a speech at the Amway arena in downtown Orlando. Afterward, we threw a big graduation party at our home with immediate family, extended relatives, friends, and neighbors that had all come to know, love, and support Joseph's development over the years. It was so special to be able to facilitate such a beautiful celebration of his young life and all that he'd accomplished. It was a perfect sendoff into the next chapter. As the end-of-the year-festivities commenced, it marked the beginning of our last three months to prepare for college.

INTENTION

I want to feel exhilaration for Joseph, my offspring, going to a school that represents excellence that will further develop him to be the kind of person he came into this world to be. This is the next step to living out his greatest ambitions and dreams. It is essential that this experience take place in order to give him opportunities he would not have otherwise.

AFFIRMATION

"There's something more for me to know here. Let me see all the facts. Let me hear guidance from within. Let me take the steps I know to take...follow the yellow brick road, knowing more information will be given to me as I go. I don't have to know how it's all going to happen. I just have to know what I want to happen...something surprisingly better than what is! Knowing it is going to be good will free me up from yet another 'thing'."

IDEAL DAY

HAPPY 1ST DAY OF SENIOR YEAR

August 17, 2015

The most amazing, fun, loving, smooth, easy, delightful last year together has begun. Everything comes together, magically by the Infinite Hand of God demonstrating ITs prowess and grandiose handiwork. Everything is perfectly planned and plays out to our satisfaction and pleasure. YOU do work with us that makes us smile forever! Joseph is stepped through the process toward the most ideal situation for him. He is absolutely in love with himself and his new life. His experiences and education carry him through life into bigger vistas and playing fields than any of us could have imagined possible. YOU are really really good at what YOU do! I can't wait to see where this goes. We have so much fun along the way and we are all absolutely free to enjoy the entire experience, including a great celebration of his 18th birthday in January and a fabulous graduation party at the end of the year with family and friends in his honor.

I love how the plan comes together for us now, including everything we could possibly need to make this happen. Make it so Universe, in the incredibly amazing way YOU and only YOU can and do. I love it!

I love YOU! I love us all!

And so it is! Thank YOU! Thank YOU!

MIND TREATMENT for SUCCESSFUL COMPLETION OF THIS PHASE

We live in a Universe of Perfection. Outstanding Intelligence permeates everything.

I am one with this beauty, magnificent, supreme Knowingness.

We are one with this Infinite Life Force that knows exactly what it is doing with us all.

Today, we are complete with this phase. We achieved getting our son to the place where he is ready to venture off into the world on his own.

Everything comes together easily, effortlessly, ...timely. We are clear, focused and the Universe orchestrates it all to perfection. Our time is well spent. We have everything we need for completion, here, today. The way is made easy for us to move through the next phase of getting him moved to Seattle.

Unlimited resources of the Universe fund our entire trip. Ultimately, Joseph's entire college expense is paid in full. We are all radically supported, debt-free, continuing to have the time of our lives. We are inspired to keep on living to the fullest. Life jumps in, making more possible – freeing us up from the old and making way for the new, the more playful, the joyful, the best life has to offer.

Today was a complete success. We have completed everything in a timely manner with plenty of time to relax before we set off tomorrow. This treatment does its divine work and returns to us multiplied abundantly!

All is well in our world!

Thank YOU! Thank YOU! I love YOU! I stay awake to this day and enjoy every minute of it!

And so it is!

DEMONSTRATIONS

The perfect school with his name on it was demonstrated

UW gave him a partial scholarship

Beautiful sendoff

We all kept our cool through the hectic, intense, long days of shopping, organizing, packing and sending things off in the mail

We are all happy about the new direction of things, (we've been ready for change!)

It's time for Joseph, John and I to follow our individual dreams

While this feels like a loss, there is a greater gain to be had

I know Joseph, as an extension of us, fulfills adventures that we will only dream of. We enjoy them, too, through him!

Our baby is headed west

His room is cleaned out

We are free to enjoy ourselves and discover our new selves and paths!

This is the successful completion of our "Base Camp" together!

Chapter Seventeen: An Alaskan Cruise

"It's my conviction that slight shifts in imagination have more impact on living than major efforts at change...deep changes in life follow movements in imagination."

— Thomas Moore

"Imagination is more important than knowledge. For knowledge is limited to all we now know and understand, while imagination embraces the entire world, and all there ever will be to know and understand."

— Albert Einstein

"Our goal should be to live life in radical amazement...get up in the morning and look at the world in a way that takes nothing for granted. Everything is phenomenal; everything is incredible; never treat life casually. To be spiritual is to be amazed."

— Abraham Joshua Heschel

"We have to do something special for our 25th Wedding Anniversary. After all, that's where it all began!" John and I wanted to go somewhere and do something that neither of us had ever done before. He suggested Alaska, and I was completely on board with that idea. We weren't really a couple that went on vacation. We traveled so much for conferences, workshops and family events that we typically didn't have time to even think about traveling for personal luxury. With so many options available, where does one begin? Of course I wanted to see spectacular natural landscapes, and yet, there had to be something more, something educational that we would have interest in that would give us even more to talk and think about. I couldn't define what it was until one day I opened an email with the subject line of Abraham/Esther Hicks Alaskan Workshop & Cruise. I went to the website. They were conducting an upcoming cruise out of Seattle through the southern passages of Alaska, with stops in Ketchikan, Juneau, and Skagway, then back to Seattle with a short stop in Victoria, BC. All this would be accompanied by a daily workshop with Abraham. This was Perfect! The trip would fit the bill for my three intentions.

MY THREE INTENTIONS

Celebrate our twenty-five years of marriage.

Allow the gorgeous landscape to take my breath away and shock me back into reality.

Seize the opportunity to have my spirit filled and renewed.

Later, I added a fourth: I wanted the trip to be paid for in advance. I really wasn't asking for much. Hearing Deepak Chopra, a well-known author and expert on metaphysics say, "Our attention fuels our intention. The deeper we go with our intentions, fleshing them out, the easier they are to demonstrate," His words further advanced my beliefs. I would find a way. If we look at ourselves as energetic beings, each having a specific vibrational frequency, I was confident that I was broadcasting a vibration synonymous with my intentions.

My four intentions, in addition to my spiritual practices, turned out to be a winning combination. Everything I wanted took place and more, starting off with an unexpected welcome almost as soon as we boarded the ship. We were greeted with a glass of champagne, and John turned to me with a toast. As he raised his glass, he said, "Here's to another 25 years together."

His words caught me so off guard, I choked. Then, he kissed me right there and then. What a perfect way to start a dream vacation! Our very first cruise! None of it seemed real!

We joined eight hundred others for a workshop every day, usually a couple of hours in length, which was just the right amount of time to think deeply inbetween our stops at different ports. John's sister, Joby (from the gator sighting), her husband, Adam, his brother, Paul, and his wife Tess came along for the ride. We got to spend precious time with them, as well as meet some new friends who we shared a table with for the first night's dinner. It turns out, they were actually current members of our original church in Atlanta. We had fun swapping stories of Kennedy Shultz and other mutual connections. One of them even knew my cousin Walter at the time.

John and I were enthralled by what we learned: Abraham's practical, loving ways of living with an advanced consciousness inspired rich, deep conversation between us. Watching volunteers "on the hot seat" talking about specific situations they were struggling with and getting clarification on how they could look at things from a higher perspective to get greater results in their lives took us all to new heights of awareness, for which we were all so grateful.

Attending the workshops together brought John and me closer, without a doubt, showed us something more to work with in our own personal lives, gave us a new shared verbiage to use to communicate, and deepened our core values. Being away from everything we knew, relaxing, soaking in all of that beauty, gave way to words I thought I would never hear from John: "I am ready to step down from the Center".

Months before, I'd decided I was done. At the time, he still wanted to hang on for a few more years. I fully supported it, but I knew in my case, twenty-five years was long enough to do anything. I felt a strong need for a change. Time was marching on. It was time for a new perspective. And now, it was John's turn.

We spent the first couple of days at sea, en route to our destination. On the third day, we witnessed what they called a catastrophic calving at Dawes Glacier. In a hauntingly glorious cacophony, enormous chunks of ice broke off and indiscriminately plunged into the waters. Though we were far enough away to watch safely, we saw many beautiful, crystal-clear, sapphire chunks of ice as the ship inched as close as possible to the main event. The naturalist aboard said they had never seen such a dramatic calving before. It was astounding, and at the same time powerfully emotional to watch such an enormous glacier break off into a thousand pieces. We constantly hear about global warming and its effects on the ice, and I knew my own actions likely played a part in this very catastrophe. It's hard not to get attached to magnificent structures and creations of nature, wanting them to stay the way they are forever. Nothing is truly all good, or all bad, or all lovely, or all sad. It is all a part of the experience. There is beauty and shadow in it all.

On Wednesday, John and I headed out with a small group. This expedition would allow us to walk up to a glacier near Skagway. As we left the ship on a small expedition boat, the winds started picking up. About thirty minutes out, the waters were so choppy that we had to turn around. A major storm was setting in. Our guides determined that it was unsafe to proceed.

I was so disappointed. It took me a few moments to process the loss. I couldn't muster a spiritual bypass and say that it was all okay, because in my book, it wasn't. I'd come all this way to have that adventure. I really wanted to experience everything that I could while I was here!

I calmed down after a few minutes and knew that ultimately, they made the right call. Our safety and lives are much more important than any sight to see. So what if we were leaving port that evening? Who said this was the right time for us to see it? Once again, I had to release an attachment. As soon as I made that shift, divine inspiration hit.

Technique: Small Shifts

I remembered Abraham, a collective of higher consciousnesses, saying at our introductory meeting that there would be some contrast that week. By that, they meant disappointments, challenges, opportunities...life? How could there not be some ups and downs where people, weather, and travel were involved? They'd taught us a technique for just such occasions to help us turn things around. We were prepared from the start before situations ever came up—as we always are in an intelligent universe.

Some things happen in our lives that are shocking, disturbing, or undesirable. When they come up, it can be hard to make the 360° turnaround from being upset to feeling good again if you don't have some good techniques. The one they shared with us was about making small shifts or taking small, 1-to-10-degree steps towards making us feel better. Sometimes it takes time for us to get to 'I am good with this', and that's nothing to be ashamed of. Even the most boat-rocking tasks can be navigated with the right equipment. This was hardly one of those situations, but this simple little exercise came in handy for me, when I did not want to miss a thing. After all, how often do you get to Alaska?

Look at this beauty that you have been immersed in for the last several days. Look at how well you have been doing on this small boat and very choppy waters. No sea sickness as in the distant past. Remember, only yesterday you witnessed a magnificent, one of a kind, glacial event. Look at these beautiful young men that are running this excursion, sharing everything they know about this vast wilderness and the history of the indigenous people in these parts.

One of the guides recommended a book, *Across the Shaman's River*, about John Muir and his experiences in the Alaskan wilderness. His exposure to the indigenous people helped him realize how advanced their culture really was. I purchased a copy of his account at the local bookstore. I love hearing about indigenous people and how they lived. It is fascinating.

By the time I got through those small shifts, I had successfully found my way back to my happy self again. I decided that next time, I would book more than just one excursion to make sure I would be covered, just in case weather was a common issue. And…you never know. Maybe it was too dangerous. Maybe we just weren't supposed to do it. Maybe we got saved.

If truth be told, I *did* have a few reservations about the expedition beforehand. Will it be too strenuous for me? Do we have the right clothes to make it through the day? What if we get wet? Summers in Alaska are freezing cold, and we were set to climb a junction about forty-five minutes out from the ship. Are we supposed to bring food?

I may not have caused the storm, but I believe that my being out of alignment played a part in the excursion not happening. In any case, the frequency I was broadcasting wasn't exactly clear! I was not broadcasting confidence, surety, or trust. Sure, I was enthusiastic, but my vibration was not in alignment with what I thought I was ready to experience, leaving me with a mixed result. Okay, Universe. Noted. Next time I will be ready!

Technique: Mutuality

Most of us seek alliance, agreement, or mutuality, with each other or with those around us. We are afraid to be different or think differently from others in a way that they might deem bad. This tendency is a part of our nature to encourage us to see harmony and connection, but it can also get in our way. We might doubt ourselves and put more weight on the opinion of one or more others who know less about us than we know about ourselves. Instead of meditating or listening to our own internal guidance, we opt to phone a family member or friend and ask what they think first. Is it really necessary that we check in with others about the average spiritual dilemma? Instead of getting external validation from our partners, friends, or family, it is important to get into alignment with our own personal, internal Source Energy first. It is from there that we can be led to the right wisdom and the correct course of action. It's hard to make the wrong move when we start from that place.

Mutuality is less about worrying what others will say and more about connection and communication with the Divine—putting God first and getting into alignment with what it is that we really want. We can give up that old habit of getting advice from others and have more fun embodying the role that we were designed to play—one of creative freedom and imagination, of listening to and following Spirit's lead. Nothing brings us into mutuality better than taking a pause, listening, being quiet, taking a rest, and shutting down the brain with its endless thinking. And mutuality can take us to places we've never been before.

As we headed back, this second technique helped with some other contrasts I encountered out on the open seas. This royal boat, the Celebrity Solstice, did all it could to handle the high winds that continued to rage throughout most of the days we were out, but the one following the glacier raincheck day was more of a challenge for me. I had a bit of a headache, and everyone had to hold onto railings and furniture to keep their balance.

My first shift in thinking took place at the breakfast buffet that morning when a young woman who I didn't know turned to me and said, "I kind of like it like this."

That was not a response I expected to hear from anyone. After that, I was able to look around and notice the miracle of how quickly people were adapting and continuing to go on about their business despite the turbulence. Clearly, it was not greatly affecting the majority of the people here. Maybe they had more experience with this than I did?

A passage came to me from the movie *Grand Canyon*, one of my favorites, where the husband (played by Kevin Cline) groans to his wife (Mary McDonnell), "I have a headache." She'd just finished telling him about the healthy newborn baby she'd found in the woods while out running that morning. She exclaims, "That's an inappropriate response to a miracle." They later fall in love with the baby and adopt it.

Sitting with family members around the breakfast table, I blurted out, "My headache is an inappropriate response to all of this wonderfulness!" They stared at me, not sure what to do with that! By lunchtime, mesmerized by the seas, I sat next to the window on the 14th floor. There I saw my first whale's tail off in the distance, amidst the white caps. It looked tiny in comparison to the huge ocean. It was nothing like the closeups we see on Nature shows, but it didn't matter, it was my first. I was ecstatic!

That afternoon, focusing on the wisdom being shared in the day's workshop, I was oblivious to the curtain on the stage of the theater swaying back and forth. With some small shifts in my thinking, and mutuality with my inner being instead of focusing on the conditions I was experiencing—plus an Aleve—I was free of any motion sickness and felt perfectly fine for the rest of the trip. I was healed. I can do the open sea!

John and I could very well have had a great cruise without all of my original intentions. How could we not? How could we not enjoy a celebration of our almost three decades worth of beautiful years together? How could we not be satisfied enough by the astonishing beauty of the natural landscape we found ourselves in? How could we not be filled with the inspiration of it all?

Yet, because I aimed at more, I got more and then some. There is great truth to the saying, "Ask and you shall receive." By setting my intentions, I got to see how much this trip really meant to John and me, both individually and as a couple, and how important it is to take care of oneself and create spaces where you can get away in retreat. Regroup. Recharge. See the world. I got to see and experience a taste of who we were together before we started this incredible life over 25 years ago. It was delightful.

Beyond my original intentions, there was so much more: From the words of encouragement each morning from our Greek Captain, Tasos, sustenance provided throughout each day by an impressive body of staff from all over the world, and some of the most delicious foods I've ever tasted to end each day. Most of all, John's timely realization that he was done with his work at our Center, in and of itself, was a game changer for us. In that relaxed, carefree setting, it became clear to him that he was complete and ready to begin again with something new. I was thrilled. Now, we were both ready for a big change.

We all get out of life what we put into it. I was enchanted by the beauty and care the Universe demonstrated throughout the whole trip, down to our very thoughts and beliefs. I felt happier, wiser, and more fulfilled than ever! The Universe enforces no limit on what we can be, have, or do. And there is more than enough for us all to experience as much as we can! It is a beautiful world!

IDEAL DAY

October 20, 2017

A beautiful, magnificent retreat away together in celebration of our commitment, life and work together – a truly amazing anomaly. Rare. Beginning with and reflecting as the spectacular Alaska. Breathtaking. Divine substance needed to make it all happen. So we can see and feel God in this way, $10,000 and beyond must be mine, ours now!

IDEAL DAY

January 26, 2018

My Ideal Day is filled with confidence, courage, peace of mind and heart, beauty, goodness, unlimited wealth, vibrant health, youthfulness, vigor, trust, clarity and focus.

I am the Great Spirit as me. I am the Radiant I AM as me.

Universe, I am ready for:

A celebration of our 25 years together – Alaska, seeing the beautiful state, with Abraham. It's powerful, enlightening, a call, with the best possible company and money to cover the trip.

Make it so in the spectacular way YOU and only YOU can and do!

I give thanks for the most ideal celebration of our marriage.

And so it is!

OMG!

What a huge celebration of our life together – it's richness, beauty, wealth and love...all the fruits of our labor. We celebrate it in the most amazing way, surrounded by beautiful people who live at a level of consciousness that is truly extraordinary. We enjoy new surroundings, relaxation, confirmation, affirmation, Big Love, and we come up and away from this experience fully expanded in new and wondrous ways. I love being out of the country—enjoying new lands and cultures. It's all very exciting!!! We are richly fed by it all, and we take our place among the gods! Heaven on Earth!

DEMONSTRATION

A fabulous trip of a lifetime to Alaska, dynamic workshops that took our consciousness to new heights together, and an unexpected $10,000 to pay for the trip.

Chapter Eighteen: Stepping Down

"The strongest position you can take is always on the side of happiness and peace as they are the Reality of our lives...you know what to do in the face of apparent distress: you persist as hard as the circumstances do, only you persist in ignoring them and living on your side of the question, that of peace, happiness, and well-being. Persistence is a wonderful manager."

— Emma Curtis Hopkins

in *Unveiling Your Hidden Power* by Dr. Ruth Miller

"Faith is a mental attitude which is so convinced of its own idea, which so completely accepts it, that any contradiction is unthinkable and impossible."

— Ernest Holmes

It isn't easy stepping down from a work that you have put all your heart and soul into, but I knew it was time. When I realized that John and I were coming up on our 25th anniversary at the Center, I knew. Life is too short. I yearned for more, even though I had no idea of what that might be. I was proud of the work that we had done throughout those two-and-a-half decades. There is so much to celebrate about who John and I are today because of that work. That is priceless. Even so, it was time to change.

IDEAL DAY

My Ideal Day is filled with enlightenment, appreciation, inspiration, financial freedom, success, wisdom, love for myself and John, order and organization, happiness, divine right action.

I am the Radiant I Am as me.

I am Spirit incarnate.

Universe in me and as me, I am ready to:

Release the responsibility of leading this community. I know this is your Center. I know there are right next steps for our own creative expression. I know different channels for divine substance open up that free us from this responsibility and allow us all to flourish and prosper. I know the center is in divine hands and now easily and effortlessly transitions into its next iteration of what YOU want to be through and as it. YOU take it where YOU want to go with it. YOU take us where YOU want to go with us. There is more for us all NOW! Guide us, show us the way. Free us all up to express YOU in the most desirable way for all. A divine solution takes place now!

Universe, make it so in the most perfect way you can.

Thank YOU for loving me, loving us, for always being here, for new direction, for the continuous expansion of consciousness, for co-creating with YOU, for our freedom, for beauty and goodness, for the best life ever, for precious time with YOU always, for movement forward.

Thank YOU for taking such good care of our children and those close to us.

I wholeheartedly accept all this and more now!

And so it is!

OMG! CARD

November 21, 2017

OMG! I am so free. I have done an amazing, incredible job these past 24 years. I have given this community, CFCSL, CSL, our families, ourselves all those around us the very best love, attention and high-mindedness...the best I could have given. I have not only helped with the transformation of thousands of lives through the years and created an extraordinary community, I, myself, have been magnificently transcended to a new order of being. It feels absolutely fabulous to know what I know, to be who I am...to have participated in the creation of the life we are living which only continues to get better and better. I am in awe of all the Universe has in store for me. The Universe continues to maximize my potential, creating circumstances and opportunities that are extremely delightful. They fill my spirit in new and exciting ways. I stand in wonder at how perfectly and precisely I have been stepped through the process of releasing this community to capable, loving individuals, aligned with our vision, mission and purpose and loved by our community as well. It is a smooth, loving, easy transition for all. Graceful. This work carries on in a strong way which makes me exceedingly happy. My life goes on richer and more wonderful than ever. Thank YOU! Thank YOU! And so it is!

IDEAL DAY

Today, I know an absolutely divine and perfect idea for the future of our center transpires—the very highest and best outcome possible takes place for all involved. We love and cherish this center. I release it to YOU now, to take care of in the way you see fit. I continue to love it and our people and watch it grow. It grows in the way it wants to grow, a way that serves more beautifully than ever. I know I am used in a way that feeds me most and allows me to give my best gifts. I am generously provided for every step of the way. I know YOU know what YOU are doing with us all. I absolutely love how YOU make something more out of all of this. GROWTH, EXPANSION and Great Love for ALL! I am, we are so blessed! Thank YOU, God, for the perfection of YOU showing up everywhere. All is well.

After our cruise in July, where John decided he, too, was complete with our work at the center, we stayed quiet about our plans for another couple of months. We wanted to make sure we knew what we were doing before involving anyone else, especially because there was no backup plan. Ideas kept coming to us on how we could improve the Center in preparation for that day when we *did* decide to leave, whether that day would be soon or not. We followed Spirit's lead.

There were no savings. We had some equity in the house, but it wouldn't last us long. As a minister, I was advised to opt out of social security in the early years, so there wasn't much there either. We would need income.

But first, spiritual preparation:

IDEAL DAY

Today is the Day!!! We share our secret with the Leadership.

My day is filled with relief, transparency, joy, laughter, freedom, fun, play, upliftment, creativity, abundance.

I am the Radiant I Am.

I am Eternal Spirit.

Universe, I am ready for:

1) *A smooth, joyful, creative, loving, healthy transition out of our work here at Central Florida Center for Spiritual Living.*

2) *Downsizing, clearing and cleaning.*

3) *Fabulous nature and beauty all around the world.*

4) *Doing what I love.*

5) *Giving in the ways I want to give.*

6) *Being true to myself.*

7) *Taking my place on the next echelon of life, discovering a whole, new world there.*

8) *Living in a really great place with high energy and beauty that feeds my soul.*

Universe, make it all so in the spectacular ways YOU and only YOU can.

I agree to dream big, totally trust and surrender to your divine plan which I already love!!!

Thank you for encouraging me to take the highest possible road and to go for the gold this round!!! I am ready. I was born to play!

Thank you for taking such care of us and this community as we go through this transition.

I wholeheartedly accept all this now and more.

Today is the day! The Truth sets us all free...already has!

At a Leadership Care meeting one morning in late September, we broke the news. We called all the key players together and told them we had an announcement to make. We had been saying we wouldn't be there forever for a couple of years now, with the knowledge that it would have to happen eventually, and with the hope that it would help ease the transition for those who might've become accustomed to and reliant on our presence at the Center. We had been empowering them to step into their own by taking more individual responsibility for the fate and future of the community. We were making decisions that not only affected those of us currently involved but also the generations who would be following us in the future.

To our delight, they took the news rather well. Being in a transient area and an aging community, there were no guarantees about any of us being there forever. Still, it was a shock to hear the final declaration come out of our mouths. It was tough to say the words we wanted to say to these beautiful beings who had helped us keep this center thriving and well for so long. It was heartbreaking for us all. We had grown so close through the years. We considered them family. A half-a-year's notice meant that we could get them ready and finish up projects we were working on, as well as prepare us all for the final goodbye. We kept true to our intention and made the most of our time together, accomplishing all we could.

Early that December, John and I decided to go car shopping. We needed a new car and figured we'd better get it while we still had a salary. Good transportation is a must. We took the steps we were directed to take. More would have to be revealed as we went.

As the year came to a close, we received a letter from a lawyer representing one of our founding members, Anna, who had passed away in the Fall. The letter opened to reveal a life insurance payout, gifting the center some money from an insurance plan. This unexpected letter marked a profound shift in the center's finances and meant they could give us some of the pension owed to us for retirement.

The strange thing about the letter was that it was dated December 25, 2018. What law office works on Christmas? We couldn't help but think Anna had something to do with that…a Christmas present from her. It brought a smile to our faces. That would be something she would have done. Our hearts were filled with tremendous thanksgiving. For John and me, this was a big confirmation that we were on the right path. We now had something to work with to get us to the next leg of our journey, even though we had no idea where that road would lead.

EXCERPT FROM AN IDEAL DAY

Thank you for moving us forward. We continue to take steps in the new direction, releasing the old everyday and embracing the new: clarifying as we go. YOU know how wonderful this all can be for everyone. YOU lead the way. We follow. I am totally open to your biggest plan. Together we take everyone to a higher level. I am yours! I love YOU so! And so it is!

A year and a half after writing my first OMG! card related to our exit in November of 2017, we had our last Sunday. People came from all over the country. Students we had through the years, friends of the center, some who had moved away, others who simply hadn't attended in a while. With our heads swirling with things to do, we didn't think to invite family until the last minute, not giving them much notice. Nonetheless, my brother Joe came in from South Carolina on the last day. Even our friends Kathy and Floyd, founders of the Outreach Program, were there, making the trip all the way from Iowa just to be with us on our special day. It was all so touching and very emotional.

We had a beautiful ceremony, passing the baton to our board of trustees, with live music by Wayne Gratz and Paradise (our home band), and a generous, lovely spread of food. Past and current members shared stories about how much we and the center meant to them, some addressed John and me directly with personal messages of love and gratitude. We received more hugs and well wishes than I had ever experienced before. John and I went home in a trance. What we had just done did not seem real.

INTENTION

To step down from this 25 year commitment in a way that was consciously loving for ourselves and our community

DEMONSTRATION

The successful completion of our 25 years as co-leaders of the Central Florida Center for Spiritual Living, and a sweet, loving farewell sendoff.

Chapter Nineteen: Back to Atlanta

"If you want to be a liberated vessel for the evolutionary impulse you must learn how to directly experience the chaos and confusion of your own mind without being disturbed by any of it. Only if you can bear it will you be able to take responsibility for it. If you can't calmly endure the chaos of your own mind, others will inevitably suffer the consequences. ...Meditation is training for life. Stillness is training for action."

— Andrew Cohen, *Evolutionary Enlightenment*

"Between stimulus and response there is a space. In that space is our power to choose our response. In our response lies our growth and our freedom."

— Viktor Frankl

During some recent visits back to Atlanta to visit my cousin Walter, we noticed that he was not his usual vibrant, energetic self. Now he was down, lonely. His companion had passed away six years prior. He was beginning to show signs of mental deterioration. Years before, he had asked me to help him with his "end of life" stuff. In recent years, he asked me to be his health advocate and executor. Of course, I said yes. He saved my life all those many years ago. I cared deeply for him.

John and I both were open to change but didn't feel we were really ready, physically and mentally, to jump into another big project so quickly. It meant we had to sell our house and move away from friends and family, who were mostly part of our center. Just when we needed a break, a new plan of action got our attention. If there was somewhere my heart wanted to go, it was the Pacific Northwest where we could be closer to our two sons and explore all of that gorgeous nature. I felt like I needed significant amounts of nature to restore my soul.

Moving back to Atlanta was the last thing I felt like doing. Besides this, Atlanta had grown tremendously in the last 25 years since we last lived there. It was huge when we left. Walter lived in Midtown. I had never lived in a city before…the outskirts yes, growing up in Milwaukee, but not in the heart of one. I was open, but my level of comfort was challenged. I remember asking him, "Do you think we can work together long-distance if we don't choose to move back?"

Graciously, he said yes, but we both knew that wasn't going to cut it. He had already begun to reach out to people he hardly knew for help. What can you really do across the country? We had already been exchanging phone calls regularly from the start. But we knew that the time was now for us to have a greater presence in his life. He needed more.

John was the first one to say it out loud, and I knew it was the right thing to do. Walter was a major player in my own journey. I wanted to be there for him. And John promised to be right there with me. What a good man he has been to stand by my side, and jump in to help wherever he was needed. With Nic and Liz, with Joseph, and now with my cousin.

It didn't take long to realize that we weren't ready to make the big move across the country yet, but if we stayed in the area, people would continue to call us and never transition to the new minister. It was a difficult position to be in. We knew Atlanta, and we were needed. This was a person who made it all possible for me…including the demonstration of John, almost thirty-four years ago. Everything I know and love about my life today began with Walter.

When I called to tell him we were moving back to Atlanta, he was floored. He just couldn't believe it. He was even more surprised that we took a small downstairs apartment across the street from him. He knew the owner, and it was very convenient to be close. As soon as we could manage it, our home was on the market.

My journal entry on May 29, 2019 was for selling the house:

I, we, have the courage, the readiness, for the new buyer to come forth. They love this house and can't wait to make it theirs. We have the courage to break out of this heaven/this home/this sacred space we have enjoyed for a quarter of a century/this comfortableness, this life we know and love AND fully trust and know that there is even more waiting for us to accept, embrace and enjoy—an even bigger life is waiting to be lived that is calling us to it!

We released all that we could and packed up the rest. The house, in a good neighborhood and school district, was a guaranteed sell, and it sold within two months. We were now ready to move to Atlanta, but not without one more glorious trip to the ocean. In our final days in Florida, our oldest, Nic, and I headed to the coast for one last swim. To our pleasant surprise, there was a cove filled with manatees galore on the intercoastal side. What a sight to behold. It was a lovefest and we took in every minute we could. We enjoyed our last hoorah immensely.

While it was far from easy to uproot us from 25 years of living in the same place, the Universe made it easy with the help of an OMG! card:

OMG!

Phase 2 of "Getting Out of Dodge" was the easiest ever. Every single detail was handled exquisitely by the Creator of worlds. Leaving our home and Florida was the right decision. John and I are thrilled with our new life, fully knowing it is better than we could ever have imagined. God's timing and solution were best for all involved. John and I are divinely placed and ready to go with new opportunities and fun adventures. We are in the greater flow. God is ON in a big way as us. This is the best life ever!

Fortunately, Walter was still very independent. Other than him having some episodes of forgetfulness every now and then, it turned out to be a very special time for the three of us to be together. We enjoyed my cousin, living where all the action is—in the city, revisiting where John and I first met. It was fun and good. Not always easy but together we took it on. We were able to enjoy rich conversations. We had weekly Friday lunches at Whole Foods which he loved, then Sunday brunches on the porch when COVID hit. We were able to be there for each other. Despite our initial reluctance to move back, Atlanta became a new adventure.

We didn't know how long we would be there, so we settled in. I finished my second book and began an interim ministry position with our center in Dayton, Ohio. We not only got to spend time with Walter, we met up with friends from the center there we hadn't seen in years. Also, our niece and her fiance had recently moved to the area. We had the privilege and honor of marrying them during that time.

We had no idea that the end was coming so quickly. Walter was gone within a year. One day, I received a call from Walter's renter that she had found him on the floor of his kitchen. He had hit his head and was down for an indeterminate amount of time. Unbeknownst to us, that was the beginning of the end. Once 911 took him to the hospital, because of COVID, we could only communicate by phone which was difficult with him having a head injury. With little contact with his loved ones, things went from bad to worse within a couple of weeks. The next time we were allowed to see him was when he was admitted to the hospice section of the hospital. We finally got some time to talk and pray together before he left. He hung on for several more days. The nurse on duty had the idea to give him a shave, getting him ready for his journey home. I wasn't surprised to get the call at 3:22 am that he made his transition. It was his favorite time of the day, and I had been tossing and turning at about that time. Now we could both rest easy knowing he was free.

IDEAL DAY - MAY 3RD, 2020

I am ready to know what is most important for us to know about Walter – to know he is getting what he needs at soul level, that his life goes the way he wants it to go, that we get to have some closure if and when that time comes. The right next steps are in place and ready to go for him.

That everyone is working together on his behalf. That we all know what we are doing. That the best solutions are implemented by the Universe, his higher self. That I, we, gave him what we were supposed to give him. Knowing his truth, his perfection.

He never wanted extraordinary means to be employed in keeping him alive. Things progressed quickly as he would have wanted. It was sad to lose such a key member of my life, but I knew he was free and happy. Walter lived fully and richly, traveled the world, and lived life on his terms. He gave his all to life and Life gave him what he needed and desired all the way to the end. He spent his last few months walking around our beautiful neighborhood, during the most magnificent springtime I have ever witnessed, appreciating it all. What he really knew about what was going on for him, we will never know. Neighbors and friends gathered in the neighborhood garden for one of the simplest and sweetest memorials I have ever experienced.

Our original intention was to be with Walter, do whatever we could to support him, and share the most important things we needed to share.

During a visit with him three years prior, I'd written the following in the form of an Ideal Day:

Thank you for the most important things to share with Walter, being in the moment during this visit; in the future, whatever is in his highest and best. Whatever we need to know, whatever we need to do, we do. This relationship continues to be mutually beneficial to us both. In fact, our remaining time together in this life is optimally spent. We have everything we need to play this out. He is perfectly and beautifully supported by YOU!

Much to my surprise, I made a list of 20 reasons why moving to Atlanta to be with him really was the right thing to do and how much we benefited from it. Life truly is never one-sided. You can't give without getting, and you definitely can't outgive God. The list continues to grow of things we gained that we never would have had or gotten to experience if we hadn't made the choice to come here and be here for him.

One of the blessings was getting to know my cousin, Barbara, Walter's older sister who lived in St. Louis. We were a team getting Walter through his last couple of weeks and then settling his estate after he passed. Much to our surprise, days after he left, she offered us his home. "He would want you to have his house."

We were speechless. It was a beautiful turn-of-the-century, craftsman-built home nestled in the Garden District of Atlanta.

John and I had no idea how all this was going to work, yet it did. This was a relationship that was set up when I was a young girl. Who would have guessed this would have played out as it did? Yes, this major detour checked so many boxes. Once we leaned into the discomfort of our grief and sadness, we could make our plans. We thought hard about leaving the house. It had many rich memories going all the way back to my earlier days in Atlanta, almost 40 years ago. It was always a place to go home to. After much thought, we decided it was time to venture out to the Great Northwest. The mountains and Puget Sound were calling us. Little did we know when we left Orlando, this detour to Atlanta would give us the means to make the move we really wanted to make with ease. Walter continues to live close to my heart. His presence is felt all around. He continues to be a bright light for all who knew him! You just never know who is going to be there for you or what you mean to someone else.

You never know where your life is going to go, but I can tell you one thing: if you hang around long enough, it gets better and better.

IDEAL DAY - SEPTEMBER 4TH, 2017

Today, I have the courage to BE myself in new ways and allow my highest and best to unfold. I yearn for adventure and am ready for it. I give my whole, entire life over to my higher Self!!! I let my Self organize, orchestrate, and order it. I take my direction from on high, knowing full well that the best life is being played out for me, for my family and for ALL! I have the courage and huge heart to follow your lead, Spirit! I boldly go where I am led, fully knowing YOU know exactly what I need and want.

Thank YOU!!! for continuing to keep me as a significant player in your big game of LIFE, all the rest of my days, doing your exquisite work!!!

OMG! - JUNE 1ST, 2019

OMG! This time since we stepped down from the center has been so fruitful. Travel, seeing family, preparing for a move and a huge life-style change, including Nic, our oldest with us for the month, has all catapulted us into a new reality. While we saw significant action steps and their results, YOU were doing so much work with us all that we didn't even see it until now. YOU prepared us and worked YOUR mysterious ways in opening us up to our greater selves and the next iteration of our extraordinary lives. YOU kept us focused and clear about our parts. YOU did the heavy lifting bringing us together, coordinating every move, orchestrating all the transitions and transformations, which freed us up for a happier, saner, more successful existence than ever! We are all so blessed. We are indeed living a special life! Thank YOU! Thank YOU!

DEMONSTRATIONS

Moved to Atlanta to be there for Cousin Walter through his transition, was given his beautiful home in the Garden District, fulfilled the terms of his will, sold his house and successfully regrouped for our next phase.

Chapter Twenty: A Special Place to Be

"The Kingdom of Heaven covers the Earth and men do not see it."

— Jesus

"At the height of laughter, the universe is flung into a kaleidoscope of new possibilities."

— Jean Houston

Now that Walter's home was sold and his estate was close to being finished, it was time to make our next big move. While we were enjoying being in Atlanta once again, COVID was going on and our friends there were hesitant to meet in person which meant there was no reason to stay. Now that my cousin was gone, the neighborhood felt empty. He was such a strong, loving presence. John and I had been through a lot in the two years since we left Orlando and our work there. By this time, we were both doing interim ministry work with different centers needing help. I was afraid that if we got too comfortable and settled there, we would never make the kind of move we thought we wanted to make. I told John, "If we are going to do this, we need to keep on moving." It takes a lot of energy to do what we did and make a big move across the country—with a cat—so we kept on going. We made our plans and followed Spirit's lead.

Now it was time for us to do what we want to do and be where we want to be. We started with spending a week in Seattle looking for a place to call home. House hunting in an area you hardly know can be a daunting task. Even though our youngest went to school here and had taken a position with a local space company, we were pretty much on our own. He was fairly new to the area himself, so he couldn't help us much.

Seattle is a huge city and area and we weren't exactly sure what area we wanted to be in. It was a difficult task, but we were up for it. After all, it is exciting to move somewhere new. We systematically drove around and inquired about interesting-looking places through Zillow. We soon learned that rental properties were going like hotcakes. You had to pretend you were interested in a place and put in your application just to see one. It was an ordeal, to say the least. By the middle of the week, we started getting discouraged.

Generally, getting what we decide we want is usually a pretty quick and easy thing for us to do. This was a whole other ball game, requiring that we bring more to the table than ever before. It seemed like the Universe had upped the ante for us during COVID. It wasn't letting us get too comfortable with how we demonstrated before. We needed a new and different strategy for this one. I knew I needed to go deeper—it's really the only answer there is to any situation or problem we experience.

Normally, John and I do most of our spiritual practices alone. This time we started treating with each other at the beginning of the day and throughout the day whenever we saw the need. We were pulling out the heavy-duty tools, (so to speak) for this one.

And …there was a bit of pressure, self-imposed of course. We were leaving to go back in a few days. We had given this first round of house hunting eight days. The good thing is that we had options. We could come back and continue the search at a later date. We could move out when our Atlanta lease was up in June and store our belongings while we rented something temporarily and continued to look. If needed, we could extend our lease in Atlanta. One way or another, we were getting on that plane, on Saturday, HAPPY! No tails dragging between our legs for us.

Midweek, I was seriously wondering what was going on. What was I missing? The realization came to me:

Of course, while there appeared to be "nothing happening", and "no progress", there had to be something else going on that I wasn't seeing. This all had to be about something more than finding a nice place to live. There is always something going on behind the scenes whether we are aware of it or not.

I realized that even in my moment of feeling disconnected—we can never truly be disconnected—I was connected.

Other gifts were being revealed as well. I was growing in consciousness with this exercise—stretching. My capacity was expanding. It was not so comfortable, but my experience was broadening. After all, we were taking on a major move, across the country, and deciding to live this portion of our lives on OUR TERMS, in a way that brought us more freedom and joy. That was huge for us!

It turns out it *was* more than finding a place to live. John and I were working together in wiser and more loving ways with each other than ever before. We have done some pretty incredible things together, like running a center and raising a child during that time. This was the expansion I asked for, which always begins with us internally first. We were being expanded. It didn't necessarily feel comfortable. Once I realized the bigger picture going on, my confidence was restored.

There were great gifts to be had that we would have missed out on if we demonstrated our new home right off the bat. We needed to:

1. Release the whole thing to God,

2. Trust the process more than ever and

3. GO WITH THE FLOW of things so it all can flow in its own perfect time and way.

Once we got to that realization, after only seeing a few places, we got on that plane to Atlanta, without a lease, with a smile on our faces, and enjoyed our adventure back. Yes, we were happy, and we calmly kept our cool for another 5 days:

1. Taking one step at a time,

2. Doing what WE COULD DO to move forward.

3. Giving our best love and attention to whatever was.

4. Sitting in the unknowing, knowing we would be led to our next steps and that there would be an ideal next place for us to live...a landing place.

On the 5th day, the Thursday morning after we got home, I woke up and decided to start my practice with a Deepak meditation which required that I turn on my phone. Normally, I don't allow myself to look at any texts or emails or listen to voicemails until I have completed my spiritual work. Nothing interferes with that quiet time!

This time, I just went right to that text button. Something else took over in me and before you know it I was reading the message. There was a text from a landlord that we had met and liked the previous week. The message read: "Let's do this!" with a smiley face.

We did find the perfect place to land! We didn't have to physically go back and search a second time or ask our son to look at places for us. We came out of this having even more experience working with the Infinite and knowing ourselves in a bigger way. That really felt good once we threw it all up in the air, released it, and let God do the heavy lifting! We were free, and that alignment kept us in the flow of what was ours, allowing it to come to us.

OMG! – March 4, 2020

OMG!!! What a year! All of the amazing growth, expansion, adventure and fun. We landed in one of the most incredible places to live, where we could see Puget Sound, Mt. Rainier, the Cascades and the Olympics. Seattle is a gorgeous place to land with inspiring views that radiate YOUR magnificence every single day. I love our beautiful, new home/place. It is clean and clear and suits us to a tee. It includes a beautiful kitchen to work and play in, a gas fireplace, spacious living areas, and great walkability central to many places we like to frequent. OMG! What a place to land! Even more exciting, it is close to our sons with a room for our daughter and the twins to visit and stay whenever they like. I absolutely love it! And we have the fiscal means to sustain it and plenty more to travel with. Life is so good! Grandeur! We are so happy!

OMG! – March 24, 2021

OMG! We landed in Seattle, on both feet, fully ready to engage in our new, big life here. We absolutely love our new home. It is practical and affordable. We have the prosperity consciousness needed to support it and be happy. The place is filled with light and love and plenty of room to relax and enjoy; it's spacious enough for John and I to do our own thing and for family to gather. We love the neighborhood and all the places to walk to. It's centrally located with lots of nature nearby. We feel good about living in the city. The gas fireplace lights up the place whenever we want to feel its warmth. The luscious private backyard feeds us. We have everything we need and more. We enjoy the presence of water nearby and the beauty of the mountains and forests. We love it all!

DEMONSTRATION

A wonderful place to land in Seattle so we can get to know the area. A centrally located home, two blocks from Green Lake. A gas fireplace that lights up when we need some sunshine and warmth. A private, natural setting for a backyard. Lots of places to walk, including restaurants and a community grocery store. Within minutes of stepping out our door, we can see the gorgeous, snow-covered Olympic mountains on the west, and on a good day, the majestic Mount Rainier. We are happy!

Chapter Twenty-One: Full Circle

"We shall not cease from exploration, and the end of all our exploring will be to arrive where we started and know the place for the first time."

— T. S. Eliot

Sacred Space

We all need time alone and we need places where we can be undisturbed by the normal interruptions of living. It doesn't matter what they look like or where they are, just as long as they are special to us and give us the time we need to renew. These are unforgettable places that feel like home to us.

Heaven knew if I was going to lead a spiritual center and have a third child, I was going to need a place nearby to be alone with my thoughts. Lake Lotus Park, a 125-acre wildlife preserve in the city—within walking distance of our home—was just the place. With an unassuming entrance that made it hard to see from the road, it was a precious hidden gem. The noises of the city faded in the distance once I walked into the park. The songs of birds deepened the silence. I loved the tranquility! This was my place to go and relax, soak in nature, feel the presence of God. It was my sacred garden. This was my escape. This incredible respite, filled with subtropical wildlife, was divinely designed just for me—part of the divine setup that would keep me centered and balanced.

The TV show *Star Trek: The Next Generation* introduced the idea of the holodeck, a 3D simulation of real or imaginary settings which the crew could create for themselves—and disappear into during their off time, while traveling through space. Lake Lotus Park became my own personal holodeck, where I could sort through what was going on, face myself, listen as the voice within me spoke words I needed to hear, think, not think…just be.

A different me emerged here among the trees as I walked through the varied ecosystems. Even the most ordinary experiences were exceptional ones. While I enjoyed the quiet, I remained on high alert for the sights and sounds of the park's creatures. I wanted to see whatever I could. Communion with nature took me deep within myself and opened me up to appreciation of being alive.

Once while walking to the park, my knee started hurting. The minute I walked into the park my knee was fine. I noticed my eye-sight was always better there, too! I always took off my sunglasses so I could see clearly whatever wanted to be noticed.

I learned to ask God, the Universe, my inner being each time: what did IT want to show me as I walked up to the entrance? What did IT want to tell me? One particular day, I noticed a butterfly fluttering in front of me on the boardwalk in the wetlands, where there was an opening for the sunshine. I extended my arm to see if it would land. For a brief moment, it did! I was ecstatic! I told it how beautiful it was and thanked it for making its presence known to me that morning.

I had many special moments there. I would see my great blue heron, owls and their babies, and hawks on a regular basis. One time, I looked up at a tree I knew to be a nest to find a precious baby owl looking down at me. On many occasions I saw alligators, and on a few rare ones, I saw bears.

One particular day, the rangers told me they had just seen the resident momma bear and her cubs heading toward the octagon, a very special place in the center of the park where I often sat contemplating my oneness with my parents, ancestors, teachers, and favorite enlightened ones. News of a sighting raised my curiosity. Quickly and carefully I headed in the direction the rangers saw her go. Not seeing her anywhere, I approached my normal seat on the octagon and to my surprise, saw thick, black hair coming through the boardwalk. OMG! Could this be? What do I do now?

I stepped back to the other side of the octagon to take a breath, but my adventuresome spirit wanted more. I couldn't resist. This was such a rare opportunity. I walked a bit farther down and looked over the railing. There she was relaxing, enjoying the breeze, her large claws resting on the ground. I felt like I had just been touched by God! Tears still come to my eyes when I think about how honored and privileged I was to be in her presence. There was no doubt that she knew I was there. Bears have a keen sense of smell. They can smell something miles away.

At one point, the city considered letting the park go. It was hard not to get upset. The rangers who poured their heart and soul into her—and who were privy to her secrets—were beside themselves. How could expanding the downtown area be a better way to spend the money?

I focused my attention on loving the park and thanking it for being there. Every time I went, I told it how much I loved it. Shortly after hearing the news, I realized that the park had its own powerful identity. It knew there was a larger purpose for which it was created. Two weeks later, all kinds of things started happening. Shifts took place in the government of the city. Out of the blue, our beautiful park became a learning center for the schools. They even considered making a mud walk for the kids. There were computers where kids could watch the animals remotely. There were so many beautiful new ideas!

Changes happened so fast. I told Frank, the ranger, "You created this." He was a teacher at heart, and he loved to talk and share about nature. I recognized him for his gift. He admitted to being that way since he was a little boy. I said, "What you were looking for is now coming to you." He confessed this was a dream, a vision he had hoped to see one day. The park expanded in its purpose and presence, affecting more lives than ever.

It helped children honor Mother Earth and gave them a way to get involved. And I got to witness a new creation.

Even though spiritual practices can take place anywhere, they are especially moving in nature. It took me a while to figure out that my whole life is my holodeck. As I create and perfect every aspect of my life, the vision of what's possible appears. My holodeck is my garden. More and more I expand my thoughts and beliefs about what it can be. With each new gyration of the picture, the Universal law goes to work on transforming its appearance. It is forever growing in lushness, brilliant colors, varieties, and breathtaking smells. Living in my garden makes me happy and fills me up.

My reality was my dream holodeck. It was peopled with amazing, incredible beings who also appreciated their time here. Everything in this world pleased me and brought me joy. I was delighted by it all. Thank you, Spirit, for the beautiful experience of these days, for supporting me so well with times to breathe and space to be in. I was renewed, replenished, and transformed. I transcended myself there, and I had the privilege of watching as the park transcended itself, too. Thank YOU for all of the sacred geometry that happened there between us. I love and appreciate YOU so much. What a wonderful life!

Everything Serves

"Everything and everyone serves," as our good friend Richard used to say. Even Brad, my first husband, played an important role in who I have become. In recent years, I had a dream that he was leading me through a dark passageway at a time when I wasn't sure where my life was going. Indeed, our 11 years together were during a time in our early development where we needed each other. We did quite well together with the limited knowledge we had in our 20s, working through some difficult times we faced. It's easy to see now that we were missing a spiritual foundation. I will forever be grateful to him for our two beautiful children, Nic and Liz.

Speaking of Nic and Liz, we always made the most of our times together. John, his brother, Paul, whom he was going into business with, and I unanimously chose a move to Orlando over North Carolina because it had fewer freeze days. Divine Providence knew Orlando also had Disney, Universal Studios and the Atlantic Ocean nearby. In addition to my visits north to spend time with my family and the kids, we made the most of their spring breaks and summer vacations by playing. My cousin worked at Disney so he was able to get us into the Disney World and MGM Studios, as it was called at the time. For a time, we went to the beach almost every weekend. Coming from the Midwest, we were all enthralled with the ocean. If we could have lived there, we would have. It was our little escape from the world. We hung out for hours, picnicking, swimming, boogie boarding, building drip castles, burying each other in the sand, and soaking in the rays. A couple of times, Nic tried his hand at surfing.

Friends I met on my Tanzania trip let us stay in their home in Vero Beach, Florida, a block away from the beach, while they spent their summers in Iowa. We walked by the sea after the sun went down, watching huge sea turtles make their way up the beach to bury their eggs. When we couldn't get away, there was the neighborhood pool a block away.

We enjoyed making our favorite foods together, too—clam spaghetti, with John's homemade Italian sauce, and seafood pizza. Once, while we were preheating the oven for chocolate chip cookies, the chips started melting in the bag we left on the back of the stove. That's how God Ugly cookies were born. To this day, we purposely create them that way! We adored our time together.

When the kids were in school and we couldn't be together, there were regular phone calls between us. The more I studied, the more I was able to share with them. They called for advice and we did mind treatments together. I was not only their mother, I took on an additional role as their spiritual advisor. I could not have planned that in a million years. It was a full circle time for me. Life was good. In reality, it was better than it had ever been. After Joseph was born and Nic and Liz were old enough to make their own decisions, they both moved in with us at different times. Today, Nick is an entrepreneur and teacher. Liz applies her nursing background in studying alternative health solutions. She loves being a Mom and homeschooling our twin granddaughters, Aubrey and Everly. They live in Wisconsin.

Shoot the Moon

Full circles seem to be the way of life. As perfect as it seemed at the time for Joseph, our youngest, to attend UW, following his dream to be on one of the premier rowing teams of the country, it did not happen. He did not make the team. We knew the stakes were high and it was a gamble. He was led to the University of Washington for other reasons; the Universe had other plans. Upon hearing the news, he went into a dark night of the soul as he tried to make sense of what he thought should have happened but didn't. He barely knew anyone there, and for the first time, he had to face this alone. I never saw him so discouraged. My only consolation was doing my own spiritual practices, which allowed me to see his wholeness, knowing that something inside of him, the larger part of him, would guide him.

It did. It didn't take him long to turn things around—only a few months. He realized that if he was going to make the best of the situation, he was going to have to get more involved with school and make some friends. While taking classes, he took on a part-time administrative position for a professor who was blind. Joseph learned how to support him with whatever materials he needed by converting them to braille. Part of his assignment was also to provide directions in braille so the professor could easily navigate his way around the campus. Thinking back now, it is easy to see they helped each other negotiate new territory, one step at a time.

Next, he joined a fraternity to increase his chances of meeting people. As he went along, he got accepted into the School of Engineering, where he became interested in Aerospace. He joined the rocket team and participated in national competitions with the rockets they built. This path led to internships with space-related companies, the last being a space company committed to building a road to space for future generations. Before the end of his final semester, they offered him a full-time position upon graduation.

As a baby, he was fascinated by the moon. As a young child, he quickly lost interest in children's books. We came home with stacks of books about space where he could dream with the pictures he saw of the cosmos.

Where does the full circle come in? Now, he spends time between Seattle and Cape Canaveral, close to our home in Orlando, where we saw dozens of rockets go up from the street in front of our house as he grew up.

The other part of that back story is that John's Dad, Al DePalma, Joseph's grandfather who he never met, worked as a Senior Systems Analyst for United Technologies in the '80s. Through their involvement, he played a part in the space shuttle program. Now, Joseph, his grandson, would also have the opportunity to work on rockets.

There was much to celebrate as it came time for his graduation as an aerospace engineer. What an accomplishment! As we started making plans to meet him in Seattle, we were disappointed to learn that there would be no graduation ceremony that year because of COVID. What do you do with that? We had all looked forward to this day. This just couldn't be. Something needed to be done. What could we do to make this occasion special? I knew I had to reach out to my higher source for ideas. In a Universe filled with infinite possibilities, there had to be a satisfying solution for us all, especially him.

Here's what I wrote on April 24, 2020, as part of my Ideal Day:

The best, most satisfying and fulfilling graduation/vacation/celebration plan comes together for Joseph. We adore him and all of us give him the honor, respect and love he deserves. It feels so good. There are perfect dates for us all to come together. Everyone shows up, present, happy and 'there for him', fully!

From that work, the idea for a Plan B emerged. We would still go out to Seattle to see him, and we would celebrate him in different ways. His brother, Nic, who lived in Portland came up and dedicated a few days to our young graduate.

One evening, we had a delicious salmon dinner with Hannah, his girlfriend, and his friend, Nick, who was visiting from Berkeley, at a famous Salmon house, Ivar's on Lake Union, with a view of downtown Seattle and the Space Needle. Restaurants were just beginning to open back up that weekend. Because so few people were going out at that time, we were able to get a reservation that day. We pretty much had the place to ourselves! It was a pleasant June evening, so of course we requested a table outside on the deck.

The four of us, Joseph, Nic, John, and I set out for a day of adventure which included taking a ferry to Bainbridge Island, driving to the Olympic National Forest and seeing Ruby Beach on the coast. We got filled up with breath-taking views of snow-capped mountains, roaring rivers, one very striking waterfall, Ruby beach on the Pacific ocean with its magnificent rock formations… AND we got to connect with each other at soul level.

It was a glorious day of celebration for us all in some of the most spectacular nature around. We laughed, we had uplifting conversations, we rested and relaxed. We enjoyed the love we share together. We celebrated Joseph: all he had done, all he was, all he was becoming.

One afternoon, we took pictures of Joseph in his cap and gown on campus along with other families making the most of the circumstances honoring their own graduates. With the help of Hannah, his girlfriend, we had a barbecue for some of his close friends. Later that evening, he got to see videos sent from family and friends who couldn't be there with us, wishing him well. Aunts, uncles, cousins and even long-time friends from our center in Orlando, who had known him since he was a baby, sent him videos congratulating him. People that we hadn't even thought to include in the original plan were able to participate by sending a congratulatory video. Next, he got to open gifts before indulging in his favorite Ben & Jerry's Cookies & Cream ice cream cake.

COVID or no COVID, it turned out to be something finer than I ever would have expected. It was heartwarming to see my family so happy.

I have to say I felt some relief that we were able to pull off a long weekend of festivities, and even more, it felt freeing to know that our son graduated and was ready to pursue his dreams. Now, he gets to work on rockets, which is a whole other story.

My intention was to have the best graduation party ever, with friends and loved ones that are there for him. It is a rich, memorable experience for us all, especially him, COVID or not. Mission Accomplished!

The Hand of God

Early on in my journey, I had the marvelous opportunity of seeing Elisabeth Kübler-Ross, a world-renowned expert on death and dying—a fiery little woman you couldn't help but love and admire.

She related a story about being late for a speaking engagement. She was on a tight schedule and as she rushed to get out of the car, she caught her hand on the door and cut it, deep enough that it bled. Her chauffeur wanted to take her to the emergency room. She wasn't having it; an audience was waiting for her. Her driver acquiesced but sat close to the front just in case she needed to leave unexpectedly.

She started right in with her subject matter, hiding her hand as much as she could. As time went on, she got so absorbed in her material, she forgot all about her hand. When she remembered, she looked down and to her amazement, her hand was healed.

How could that be? How could she have such a spontaneous healing? First, she believed she could. Second, she gave no attention to what was wrong because her thoughts and speech were focused on sharing her beautiful work with others. Amazing, isn't it? The show must go on, and it did!

Someone once asked her, "Do you notice any strange things happening in your life?" She replied, "All day…every day!" Hearing her speak made me realize right there and then, that was the kind of life I wanted, too! I wanted a life filled with happy surprises, unexpected happenings and extraordinary blessings.

Well, that's what I got! Seemingly strange, wonder-filled things catching me off guard, getting my attention, reminding me that I am a part of something much larger than myself, that I am alive in an interactive, responsive Universe, and that there is so much more to this world that I want to get to know and experience.

In Closing

Closing Letter

"The secret of change is to focus all of your energy, not on fighting the old, but on building the new."

— Socrates

"The best use of life is to invest it in something that outlasts it."

— William James

Dear Ones,

I wrote this book to share my experiences, experiments really—to offer you a picture of what you, yourself, can do with your own personal life. We are given these wonderful lives, and often we don't have a clue about what is going on. A few people hit the ground running, knowing what they want, and there is no stopping them. Others of us take a while. We have to find our way. Much of my early years were learning by trial and error and a process of elimination—trying this and that. Want this. Don't want that. Onto the next. In my 20's I wrote on a cocktail napkin 20 different jobs I had already tried and wanted to have nothing more to do with. I liked working and being with people, but the jobs were incredibly boring. I was beginning to doubt whether I would ever find work I loved. I was beginning to think it didn't exist. This work in consciousness has been the most captivating work because it continues to lure me into wanting to learn and be more.

It is my dream that these ideas will open you up to new possibilities. Starting with what we have done and who we are, and looking back on our lives from a higher vantage point, helps us to see what we may have missed and what is already in place, waiting for us.

The ideas that are included herein are founded on ancient wisdom. They go back to a time before Jesus was born. This wisdom was known by the great thinkers of all times. The interpretation of my personal experiences is purely my own and cannot be confirmed by anyone else. It is my interpretation of events from my understanding of who I am. No one can see your life as clearly as you see it yourself. From the outside, you may be able to see things I have missed about myself and what has happened in my life, but no one can see our life experiences in just the same light as we can.

If we live from the inside out, we have to pay attention to what is coming to us. We must continue to be on the alert for new ideas and dreams. There is no one like us.

We are unique in all the Universe. Others may not understand our point of view and that is okay. We are all a piece of the puzzle, and we each represent an aspect that only we can represent. Somehow all the pieces of the puzzle come together into one magnificent truth. As infinite and eternally expanding spiritual beings, we will always have more to understand and appreciate about ourselves and our relationship with Life.

I have asked for a larger than life experience. Like I said many years ago when Elisabeth Kübler-Ross told of healing her hand, I am living that life today. I want to push the envelope and know what can be done. With that comes a greater consciousness, more responsibility, and lots of forgiveness for the mistakes I have made and anyone I may have hurt along the way. Yes, as you probably already know, life comes with lots of mistakes, especially when you are stretching out of your comfort zone and trying new things. This requires a greater capacity to love yourself and everyone else, too. I expect if you are reading this book, you, too, are seeking the life you dream of. Exciting, isn't it? It's time to embrace what Life has in store for us. It's time to use our lives wisely and invest in a way of life we can pass on to our children.

It's time to celebrate the exquisite, eternal beings we are. Nothing that takes place in this world can disturb our innermost being, our essence. We are invincible Spirit!

The best is yet to come!

Love,

Cath

Acknowledgements

To my readers: my sister-in-law, Joby Burrows, my niece, Nicole Cendrowski, and my friends, Colette Marcetich Biltz, Carol Goodman and Cynder Sims Verheyen. Thank you all for giving your love and support by giving this book a closer look.

For a beautiful and lovely spirit, Jessiah Anderson, my first editor, who helped me be transparent and flesh out my feelings in a bigger way than I have ever been able to do before. For the beautiful spirit, Clay Smith, who took over as editor and brought the book into its final form. For Michael Terranova, previous publisher of Wise Women Press, who has helped bring my first two books into print. For Dr. Ruth Miller and Portal Press, my new publisher, for making this book a reality.

Thank you, John, our children, grandchildren, family, friends and ALL! I could not do this work without your undying love and support.

About the Author

Cath DePalma, a pioneer in the study of metaphysics, has dedicated her life to working with Universal Principles and practicing how they work in real-life situations. She has a great understanding of how Life works and what is needed to experience exceptional results. It is from her own life lessons, discoveries, years of life experience, and expertise that she teaches and guides others in a fun, loving way. This inspires and empowers them to experiment with these principles in their own lives in order that they may come to know themselves in a deeper way and have a closer relationship with Spirit.

For the past 30 years she has counseled, coached and encouraged thousands of people from all over the world, with various backgrounds and beliefs. For 25 of those years, Cath and her husband, John, co-directed the Orlando-based Central Florida Center for Spiritual Living. A motivational speaker, teacher and writer, Cath has a unique gift for working with others as they move through transformation. In addition to this book, she is the author of *I Can Do This Thing Called Life and So Can You!* and its beautiful companion workbook, *Energize Your Creative Powers*. Currently, she is working with spiritual leaders and communities under transformation and supporting Outreach Program's schools for children in Tanzania. She is available for speaking, workshops, and private consultations.

Contact Cath DePalma by email: Cathdepalma3@gmail.com

People, Movies and Books to Enlighten and Inspire

Quoted in this Book

Socrates – A Greek philosopher from Athens, known for his Socratic method of question and answer. Remembered for his saying, "The unexamined life is not worth living" and for his theory that if a person is not good it is because they lack knowledge.

Jean Houston – A world-renowned scholar, philosopher, futurist and researcher in human capacities and social change. One of the founders of the Human Potential Movement. One of the foremost visionary thinkers and doers of our time.

Hopi Elder – The Hopi Tribe is a sovereign nation located in northeastern Arizona and one of the oldest living cultures in documented history. They migrated north in the 12th century. The Hopi way is peace and goodwill, spiritual knowledge, adherence to religious practices and responsibility as stewards of the Earth.

Helen Keller – An American author and educator who was blind and deaf. She was an activist for physically challenged people.

Rumi – A great Sufi mystic and poet in the Persian language. He profoundly influenced mystical thought and literature throughout the Muslim world. He believed life should be a journey to union with the one true God. He taught peace and tolerance. Famous quote: "Do not feel lonely, the entire universe is inside you."

Elisabeth Kübler-Ross – A Swiss-American psychiatrist and pioneer in near-death studies.

Viktor Frankl – An Austrian neurologist and psychologist, known for the quote, inspired by his experiences in a concentration camp during World War II,

T.S. Eliot – An American-English poet, playwright, literary critic and author.

"Everything can be taken from a man but one thing: the last of the human freedoms – to choose one's attitude in any given set of circumstances, to choose one's own way."

Emma Curtis Hopkins – A New Thought spiritual teacher and leader.

Henry David Thoreau – An American naturalist, essayist, poet and philosopher.

Ernest Holmes – The founder of Science of Mind, New Thought writer, teacher and leader.

Joseph Campbell – An American writer and professor, famous for his studies on Mythology

Genevieve Behrend – A French born author and teacher of Mental Science.

Wallace D. Wattles – An American New Thought writer.

Ester Hicks/Abraham – An American inspirational speaker, channeler and author.

Vernon Howard – An American spiritual teacher, author and philosopher

The Talmud – The primary source of Jewish religious law and theology

Leonardo da Vinci – A Renaissance genius who revolutionized art and science with his masterpieces.

Thomas Moore – An Irish writer, poet and lyricist

Albert Einstein – A German-born theoretical physicist, famous for the theory of relativity.

Abraham Joshua Heschel – A Polish-American Rabbi, professor of Jewish mysticism, author, philosopher and leader in the civil rights movement.

Andrew Cohen – An American spiritual teacher and author

Jesus – A First century Jewish preacher and religious leader.

Some of My Favorite Movies

A Beautiful Mind

Apollo 13

Castaway

Defending Your Life

Eat, Pray, Love

Field of Dreams

Freedom Writers

Grand Canyon

Hidden Figures

Nyad

Pay It Forward

Shirley

Spirit

Star Trek, The Next Generation – TV series

The Boy Who Harnessed the Wind

The Great Debaters

Way of the Peaceful Warrior

Wild

The following include some violence, (for which I often have to leave the room), but the conversations between the wizards are brilliant:

The *Harry Potter* series

The Lord of the Rings trilogy

Recommended Reading

Becoming – Michelle Obama

Braiding Sweetgrass – Robin Wall Kimmerer

Brave the Wild River – Melissa L. Sevigny

Busting Loose from the Money Game – Robert Scheinfeld

Callings – Gregg Levoy

Change Your Thinking Change Your Life – Wayne Dyer

Conscious Loving, The Journey to Co-Commitment – Gay Hendricks, Ph.D., & Kathlyn Hendricks, Ph.D.

Eat, Pray, Love – Elizabeth Gilbert

Evolutionary Enlightenment – Andrew Cohen

15 Commitments of Conscious Leadership – Jim Dethmer

Leave Only Footprints – Conor Knighton

Meta Human – Deepak Chopra

Nonviolent Communication – Marshall B. Rosenberg, Ph.D.

On Death and Dying – Elisabeth Kübler-Ross

Power of Decision – Raymond Charles Barker

Reflections on the Art of Living: A Joseph Campbell Companion – Diane K. Osbon

Living the Science of Mind – Ernest Holmes

Science of Successful Living – Ernest Holmes

The Art of Allowing – Ester and Jerry Hicks

The Art of Deliberate Creation – Ester and Jerry Hicks

The Big Leap – Gay Hendricks

The Blue Zones of Happiness – Dan Buettner

The Call – Oriah Mountain Dreamer

The Dynamic Laws of Prosperity – Catherine Ponder

The Four Agreements – Don Miguel Ruiz

The Four Pivots, Reimagining Justice, Reimagining Ourselves – Shawn A. Ginwright, Ph.D.

The Myth of Normal – Gabor Mate' MD

The Places That Scare You, A Guide to Fearlessness in Difficult Times – Pema Chodron

The Power of Now – Eckert Tolle

The Road Back to You, (Enneagrams) – Ian Morgan Cron & Suzanne Stabile

The Secret Spiritual World of Children – Tobin Hart, Ph.D.

The Universal Christ – Richard Rohr

The Untethered Soul – Michael A. Singer

The Vortex – Esther and Jerry Hicks

The Yugas, Keys to Understanding our Hidden Past, Emerging Energy Age & Enlightened Future – Joseph Selbie & David Steinmetz

This Thing Called You – Ernest Holmes

Unveiling Your Hidden Powers – Dr. Ruth Miller for Emma Curtis Hopkins

You Can Heal Your Life – Louise Hay

Zero Limits – Joe Vitale and Dr. Hue Len

Addendum

Spiritual Tools Worksheets

My Ideal Day

Date: _____

My ideal day is filled with:

_____
_____
_____
_____

I AM:

_____
_____
_____

SPIRIT or Universe, in me, as me and around me, I am ready to experience the following:

_____
_____
_____
_____
_____

MAKE IT SO in a special way that only you can.

I follow my inner guidance and take the next action steps I know to take:

_____
_____
_____
_____
_____
_____

I AM grateful for:

_____
_____
_____

I AM grateful for highest and best happening for: (others)

_____
_____
_____

I WHOLEHEARTEDLY ACCEPT ALL THIS and MORE. ....AND SO IT IS!!!

Mind Treatment

Topic or Desire (What you want to do, have or be)
_____
_____

Recognition (There's only one creative power, everywhere equally present)
_____
_____
_____

Unification (I am... embodying those same attributes)
_____
_____
_____

Affirmation/Realization (That which I desire has already been given)
_____
_____
_____

Denial (anything unlike what I desire has no power in itself or in my life)
_____
_____
_____

Reaffirmation (so I can have it)
_____
_____

_____
_____

Gratitude (I'm grateful to know it)

_____
_____
_____
_____

Release (I don't have to know how to do it, I let go, let God figure out the how)

_____
_____
_____
_____

And So it is!

Other Books by Cath DePalma

I Can Do This Thing Called Life – And So Can YOU!

Energize Your Super Powers – 7 Ways to Spiritual Fitness

Related Titles at Portal Center Press

Journey to the Eye of the Heart – A Spiritual Odyssey of Hope, Faith, and Love
by Marcia Sutton

Unlocking the Power of The Secret – 10 Keys to Transform Your Thoughts & Life
by Ruth L. Miller

www.ingramcontent.com/pod-product-compliance
Lightning Source LLC
Chambersburg PA
CBHW081449070526
44586CB00019B/2278